1987

Teaching English

*Reflections on
the State of the Art*

HAYDEN ENGLISH EDUCATION SERIES

ROBERT W. BOYNTON, *Consulting Editor*

Teaching English

Reflections on the State of the Art

Edited by

STEPHEN N. JUDY

Department of English
Michigan State University

for
The Michigan Council of Teachers of English

HAYDEN BOOK COMPANY, INC.
Rochelle Park, New Jersey

Library of Congress Cataloging in Publication Data

Main entry under title:

Teaching English.

1. English language—Study and teaching—Addresses,
essays, lectures. I. Judy, Stephen N.   II. Michigan
Council of Teachers of English.
PE1065.T43   420'.7'1073   79-17965
ISBN   0-8104-6041-6

1	2	3	4	5	6	7	8	9	PRINTING
79	80	81	82	83	84	85	86	87	YEAR

Introduction

> Now, it is clear that the decline of a language must ulti-
> mately have political and economic causes; it is not due
> simply to the bad influence of this or that individual
> writer. But an effect can become a cause, reinforcing the
> original cause and producing the same effect in an inten-
> sified form, and so on, indefinitely. A man may take to
> drink because he feels himself a failure, and then fail all
> the more completely because he drinks. It is rather the
> same thing that is happening to the English language. It
> becomes ugly and inaccurate because our thoughts are
> foolish, but the slovenliness of our language makes it
> easier for us to have foolish thoughts. The point is, the
> process is reversible.
>
> —George Orwell
> "Politics and the English Language"

George Orwell probably had as much respect and concern for the
English language as anyone around. His "Politics and the English Language," written in 1945, is remarkably current in its analysis of the mis-
use of language. Orwell was equally sensitive to the relationship between
language and thinking, and his futuristic novel, *1984*, is unique in its
exploration of the use of language as a means of mind control.

When many of us first read *1984*, that date seemed far in the future.
Now we are living in the closing decades of the twentieth century, and
we can be thankful that many of Orwell's predictions have not come true.
For instance, unless the political climate changes overnight, we will not
have a "Big Brother" watching our every move through a network of
spies and telescreens. Yet if we take "Big Brother" as a metaphor for
technological capability to oversee our actions, Big Brother is already
here in many forms: in computers that keep track of our Master Charge
and Visa expenditures and thus provide electronic surveillance of our
financial lives; in a telephone network that lets us dial direct anywhere
on the globe, yet allows Ma Bell to listen, undetected, to "selected" conversations to "monitor the quality of service" (and God knows what else);
in testing conglomerates that exercise enormous control over people's
futures yet are shrouded in secrecy and accountable to no one; and, of
course, in Watergate, which should have cured us all of our it-can't-
happen-here overconfidence.

The essays in this volume are directed toward Orwell's twin concerns for the improvement of English and society, though from the perspective of English teachers rather than that of a novelist/journalist. In planning the volume, I asked each contributor to review the state of the profession and to give his or her thoughts on priorities for education in general and English teaching in particular. I offered the writers wide latitude in the form of their contributions and encouraged them to use alternative modes of discourse to the essay while exploring alternatives for English.

My own opening essay sets the stage by describing some of my "Dreams and Nightmares" for the future of our profession. It is followed by "A Foresight Saga," by Frank Ross, assessing the forces operating against successful growth in our profession, but confirming the critical importance of the well-informed teacher, one who can recall tradition as well as think about the future. Robert Graham, in "Yesterday, Today, and Tomorrow," covers some eighty years, examining his own education, current conditions, and historical roots in the nineteenth century, then uses these data to create a vision of the future based on his conception of shifting power centers in education.

The next three writers are concerned with the individual teacher. Stanley Cook's essay, "Who Aims at the Middle," might be subtitled, "What Makes a Good Teacher?" He discusses the values, attributes, and knowledge of the successful teacher, new or experienced, and describes some marks of good teaching that will be as valid twenty or fifty years from now as they are today and were yesterday. Ken Macrorie interviews a good teacher—John Bennett—whose commitment offers a model of "An Intense Teacher." Henry Maloney's "Assignment 6" defies easy classification, but its topic is Orwellian: a concern for preserving human values —and wit—in an age that increasingly grants its rewards to teachers of "the functional."

Discussing the "content" of the English curriculum, Mildred Webster reviews the ways in which the study of classics and contemporary literature can be comfortably combined as "The Basis for Curricular Design." Her article helps to show the extraordinary richness of materials and ideas that have been and will be used in fully dimensional English programs. Jean Malmstrom, in "Future Grammar," discusses our "national mania" for correctness and moves on to show how the principles of language study can be used not to oppress students but to enrich their understanding of "Grammar through Literature." In "Talkin' and Testifyin' About Black Dialect," Geneva Smitherman is concerned as much with human values as she is with language, calling for instruction that stresses individual use of language rather than shallow discrimination against speakers and writers of any race or culture because of the ways they use language.

The final two contributors focus on matters that move beyond immediate concern for what we teach toward the society in which we teach it. Patricia Fox's essay, "Separate Peaces," offers insights into school-community relationships; she provides some schemes and tactics for dealing with the public that range from the imaginative to the refreshingly outlandish. Jonathan Swift's essay discusses "The Demise of the English Department," not as a eulogy to a dead institution but as a prolegomenon to the evolution of English as an interdisciplinary, humanistic study.

Readers will note that all the contributors are or have been teachers in the state of Michigan. The state is unique in having a large number of educators who have been intensely involved in statewide educational problems, yet who have also distinguished themselves as writers and speakers on the national scene. As Publications Chair for the Michigan Council of Teachers of English, I have long wanted to collect the ideas of these people—the Maloneys, Macrories, Websters, Smithermans, Malmstroms. I am especially grateful to John Fox, past president of the council, for encouraging me to pursue the idea. I also want to express thanks to Robert Boynton of Hayden Book Company for sensing the potential of these Michigan writers to offer commentary on national concerns in English education. It should be recorded, too, that the writers have assigned all royalties from the sale of the book directly to the Michigan Council of Teachers of English.

The essays in this book do not offer either a homogeneous view of our current situation or a programmatic set of priorities for the future of English. Nor in planning the collection did I suspect or even hope that they would. Future-casting is extraordinarily difficult, and the prophets who would give us clear-cut solutions to our problems are often near-sighted, overconfident, or downright fraudulent. The eleven contributors to *Teaching English* offer us eleven unique points of view based on a collective total of nearly three hundred years of teaching. The priorities they insist on and the alternatives they propose seem to me well worth exploring.

STEPHEN N. JUDY

Okemos, Michigan

Contents

Teaching English

*Reflections on
the State of the Art*

The Future of English:
Dreams and Nightmares

STEPHEN N. JUDY

Shortly after I initiated correspondence with the authors of this collection of essays, I began to worry about what my own contribution might be. Since I didn't major in Prophecy in college, I had a sleepless night, and not unlike Ebenezer Scrooge, I was visited in consecutive hours by two Ghosts of Education Future, each giving me a vision of English teaching in the year 2001.

The first ghost was a dreadful creature with the face of my high school English teacher, a face powdered white with chalk dust, who entered my bed chamber dragging a chain of oversized paper clips and moaning about a misplaced modifier. The ghost revealed that by the year 2001 the battle over basics had been fought . . . and won . . . by the proponents of "basics." A series of taxpayer revolts in the late 1970s, coupled with rising inflation and continually high levels of unemployment, threatened the very existence of the schools. As a way of curtailing expenses and satisfying belligerent parents, more and more administrators turned to the concept of accountability, a move which took responsibility off their shoulders and placed it on the teachers'. Pressure to eliminate frills and get back to "traditional" education led to the dominance of basic skills courses in all areas.

The B. F. Skinner High School opened its doors in September of 2001 (the very week that Educational Testing Conglomerate announced that, for the 37th year in a row, SAT verbal scores had declined). Skinner had been built, in part, with federal funds for Fundamental Demonstration Centers, and even *Newsweek Micromag* sent a reporter to see what the new school had to offer.

Entering students at Skinner were subjected to four weeks of testing in the basic skills of reading, writing, visual literacy, mathematics, computer science, physics, astronomy, psychocybernetics, and hygiene. Electronic answer sheets were evaluated instantly by computers, and the test scores were sent to a central data bank deep in the soil beneath Princeton, New Jersey, for comparison with universal norms. Students whose scores were deficient were programmed into the Pavlov Remedial Wing of Skinner High, and their former teachers were sent telegrams announcing termination of their employment by the school district. At Skinner High, *everybody* was to be average or above, and failure was not to be tolerated.

Those students who met or exceeded norms for their age, sex, religious upbringing, state of health, and cultural or ethnic background were scheduled into a series of sequential, incremental, skill-objectivized learning booths, each run by a teacher selected from among thousands of applicants for his or her particular skill at teaching one single behavioral objective, say:

> The student shall master the dative absolute so that he or she shall be able to identify properly eight of ten such structures from selected passages of the King James Version of the Bible.

Students progressed at their own rates through the booths, but elapsed time of booth occupancy and skill mastery were monitored and compared to universal norms for "teacher instructional efficiency." Teachers whose students had habitually long booth occupancy times were replaced by new teachers, who had been waiting in one of the bullpens established by the teacher training institutions, where they kept themselves warmed up and in shape by teaching each other abstruse and sophisticated skills of Medieval Latin. . . .

At this point, I awoke shouting, "No, no! I can't stand it. Spirit, show me no more." Thinking this must have been brought on by the tacos or the cheap wine, I disentangled myself from the bedclothes, took a couple of Alka Seltzers, and dozed off again, this time to experience a more positive vision.

The second ghost—a stylishly dressed creature whose natural leather briefcase I coveted—revealed that by the year 2001 the battle over basics had been fought and the differences among parents, administrators, and teachers resolved. The taxpayer revolts of the 1970s and the public outcry for more basics had led to numerous school-community meetings. English teachers had been at the forefront in helping parents translate their concerns into programs that incorporated the better features of the "new education" (and eliminated some of its faddish elements) and those of "traditional education" (minus many of its harmful and obsolete notions about how children learn). Such discussions had been catalyzed by tax law reforms that led to the abolition of property tax bases and annual referenda as well as by increasing recognition on the part of the general public that good education is worth spending money on.

The John Dewey Community Learning Center opened its doors in September of 2001 without much fanfare at all. It had been funded not by federal monies but by taxpayers who simply wanted to create the best school they possibly could for their community. Although the Dewey Center was designed chiefly for the education of the young, it counted among its students a fair number of adults, many of whom served in the capacity of teacher-learner, enrolling in some learning modules while teaching others.

New students at Dewey spent their first several weeks in a series of small groups and individual conferences. Counselors and subject-matter teachers described the range of learning experiences available at the center and reviewed the student's past achievements as indicated in his or her Experience Portfolio, a permanent file of the student's past work with evaluation of that work by previous mentors. On the basis of these meetings, each student set up a program of studies, to be reviewed and revised periodically during his or her tenure at the center. Counselors could afford the time for this extensive interviewing because they no longer wasted time keeping files of standardized test scores and grades (a change hastened by the Great Princeton Data Bank Collapse of 1991). At the Dewey Center, students were not *average* or *above average* or *below average;* they simply *were,* the need for comparisons having evaporated with the demise of the grading system and nonindividualized education.

Although in the 1970s magazines like *Newsweek* had gloomily predicted the decay of language and the death of literacy, in fact The Word was alive and well in 2001, and literacy was the central and dominant concern of the new school. The "behavioral objective" of the Dewey Center was a simple, yet extraordinarily complex one: to help students learn to send and receive messages of as many different kinds in as many different modes of discourse as possible. Messages could be about science or math or history or psychology or oneself. Discourse modes actively "taught" included writing, video, drama, laser, and day-to-day conversation.

Following the now-ancient writings of Dewey himself, the teachers in the school were committed to a philosophy of learning-by-doing. The English elective courses of the 1970s had evolved successfully into interrelated topical and thematic learning clusters, most interdisciplinary, taught by several teachers who participated in the learning process themselves. The notion of a "class" and "courses" having disappeared long ago, the students found themselves working variously in small groups and large, independently and under the direction of tutors. Much of the work was done off campus—in businesses and industries, in museums and theaters and libraries, in hospitals and parks for the elderly —since the projects were designed to be of use to somebody, including the learner.

"Spirit, show me more," I cried out in my sleep, "and, more to the point, what can we educators do to bring this vision to pass?" But it was too late. The spirit was due at its brush-up course on computer languages and departed, leaving me to my contemplations in the gray light of dawn.

Of course, a third version of English 2001 is possible, a vision in which the schools look much like the schools of today, just as in substance, if not in surface appearance, today's schools bear a disturbing resemblance to the schools of the 1890s, 1920s, and 1950s. But I would like to see education move in the direction of the John Dewey Center, and I'm convinced that teachers today have the know-how to make dramatic and important changes in the schools. Nothing in my description of the Dewey Center is something that couldn't be done in our schools starting *tomorrow,* but there are some big "ifs" standing in the way, mostly "ifs" implied in my description of the forces that created the technologically sophisticated but pedagogically reactionary Skinner High School.

The second ghost was wise to duck out when he/she did, for there is no magic or easy route to the future. However, I want to suggest a process that I have found useful in working toward goals. It's called
IDEA(L)ISM AND SUCCESSIVE APPROXIMATION.
It follows a three-step procedure:

1. *State your idea(l) in detail.* I'm uncomfortable with the popular connotation of "idealism," which means "naive" or "foolish" or "impractical." Perhaps at no other time in American education has "idea(l)-ism" been more important. The Dewey Center is a general description of many of my ideals for education: a broadened concept of literacy, skill in the use of language seen as central to all education, the abolition of grades and standardized test scores, individualized learning and counseling, interdisciplinary studies, involvement of teachers in learning, and so on. In Step 1 of the approximation, *you* describe *your* visions—your idea(l)s—in as much detail as possible, at this point not worrying about whether you are being "practical" or not.

2. *Analyze the obstacles to realizing the ideal.* This is relatively easy to do, for there are many, many obstacles—lack of money, lack of interest, lack of time, lack of support, to list but a few. Barriers to achieving the Dewey Center include lack of public understanding of and support for education, administrative indifference to the substance of teaching, overcrowded classes, poorly trained and apathetic colleagues, and so on. The important part at this stage is not to become so discouraged by the obstacles that you give up the original ideal. Most crucial is that you make yourself a *realistic* list of the barriers to success, that you identify the "opposition" in writing.

3. *Devise solutions that let you approximate your ideal as closely as you can, taking the obstacles one at a time.* For example, although

interdisciplinary teaching of writing (one ideal) may not seem practical because of the many demands placed on other teachers, one can:

- provide English department writing consultants to other departments
- sponsor a faculty meeting devoted to techniques for teaching writing in all classes
- set up tutoring and volunteer centers where students can get help with their writing
- teach students ways to analyze and solve their subject-matter writing problems

Here is an example of "Idea(l)ism and Successive Approximation" at work. I recently observed a class for First American students at South High School, Minneapolis, Minnesota. The teachers had "tried everything": using Indian literature, emphasizing free reading, inviting students to explore their own cultural backgrounds. Nothing worked. The class still represented "school" to the students, who remained uninvolved. The teachers felt that a less structured setting was important for these students, who couldn't or wouldn't work in a "usual" course. Yet, the school administration wasn't much help, having come down hard on electives and modular scheduling a year earlier. Faced, then, with a conventional curriculum setting, the teachers sought a way to approximate their ideal. They hit on a solution with the help of a cooperative art teacher, who had faced the same problem with these students. Without giving the assistant principal apoplexy, they managed to schedule two English classes and an art class for these students all at the same hour. They now had three rooms, three teachers, and many students, but this scheduling introduced flexibility that allowed them to individualize. The day I visited, some students were pursuing art-English projects in the art room; others were working on English (and art) in one of the English classrooms; still others were doing individual reading; and a fourth group was interviewing an elderly member of the community.

It wasn't an ideal learning situation, and not all of the students were deeply involved. But it looked to me a lot like the Dewey Center and gave a positive example of what teachers can do in "the real world" when they keep their ideals firmly in mind.

The future, it has often been remarked, is very little more than a projection of the present. In teaching English, our future depends very much on our willingness to imagine the desirable and to attempt the possible—starting *today*. "Idea(l)ism and Successive Approximation" allows one to make plans for the future with more than a ghost of a chance for success.

Grow Old Along with Me!
The Best Is Yet to Be—
Or A Foresight Saga

FRANK E. ROSS

In the summer of 1977, the Arthur D. Little Company, a "think tank" at Cambridge, announced that within eight years the American public would no longer go to movie theaters. Instead, nearly everyone would own a device similar to the Sony video tape recorder which would permit the insertion of film cassettes into the family television set. These cassettes would be purchased in local stores or rented from libraries. Naturally, this prediction threw the theater owners of America into a frenzy. But interestingly enough, their protests and denials did not center on whether this would come to pass, only on whether it would take effect in so short a time.

That seems to be the key concern as we look at the changing climate of English teaching. Not, will change come, but will it be upon us so soon? Please, Lord, need it be so fast? Can't you let me retire before I have to recycle myself?

Cycle, of course, is really what we can expect. Fasten your seat belts; we're going around again! The period prior to the Columbia Teachers College progressive movement in the late 1920s is beginning to look attractive again. When the child-centered curriculum came in, something had to give way. Now we know it was the skills and cultural heritage that took a back seat. But as with a coiled spring, the circle does not bring us back precisely to where we were, but only in the neighborhood, yet farther ahead.

Just how far ahead we are will be calculated by technology, and by technology's child, the professional administrator. He may not have formulated a philosophy of education, but he will have cost accountants to advise him in the management of English teaching. Together they will make determinations that will affect what is taught, by whom it is taught, and when and if it is taught.

6

The professional administrator will be pragmatic if nothing else, and sometimes he will be nothing else. If a field trip or a classroom project or a teaching material brings tangible results, it will be good; if it does not, it will be bad. Whereas in previous centuries God was the reason given for preventing teachers from accomplishing some of their aims, in the years ahead it will be "the budget" and its keeper, the professional administrator.

David Cylkowski, at Detroit's Mercy College, may be right in divining that back in 1958 the planet Proademia was inadvertently struck by an early Russian sputnik. This caused Proads to abandon their globe and migrate to Earth. Although they immediately took courses in professional administration, they grew homesick for Proademia, the planet completely enveloped in darkness. So they tried to recreate it here. That may explain the fuzzy-jawed administrators of the future, branding literature courses as frills, and giving out programs of two study halls, back-to-back, and lunch during the second hour.

As soul-trying as that may be, Al Jolson would say, "You ain't seen nothin' yet." The professional administrator will usher in the electronic classroom in the modular building—not as an improvement in working conditions or as a superior means of teaching concepts, even though it may bear those labels for the public, but as a more fiscally responsible way to process students through the mandated number of school years.

A legend persists that if the original Henry Ford disagreed strongly with a staff member, he would have the man's office furniture moved into the hall at night. When the outspoken one came to work the next day, he would see another name on his door. That is why, the story goes, the grandson, Henry Ford II, built the new World Headquarters twenty-five years ago with movable office walls. Now a disagreeable man may find upon coming to work that the adjacent offices have expanded on both sides of him and his space no longer exists at all. In the not-too-distant future, this concept may have influenced school architecture to the extent that all new buildings will be modular. When enrollment decreases, a whole wing can be transported to a more populous area. This also means that a faculty displeasing the principal may find that its work-coffee room has disappeared and that now the janitor's closet has bookshelves and two chaise lounges. With this kind of easy mobility, one of the former aggravations should be gone. Each instructor will have his or her own room—can this be a trend toward the decline and fall of the roamin' teacher?

As George Orwell recognized trends in 1948, such as the telescoping of words, the shifting of connotations, the contradiction of statistics, and foreign policy by anonymous fiat, there are trends that are firmly enough established already to permit futurists like Buckminster Fuller and Alvin Toffler and the Arthur D. Little Company to prognosticate. Prognostication is the social science of extrapolation—the natural extension of known variables beyond their present limits. All we have to do is look around us at new and recent developments, and, Orwell-like, determine which ones we think will survive and mutate into something really ghastly.

It doesn't require a Plexiglass ball to took backward to see that the statute of limitations has run out on the halcyon days of English teaching in the 1960s and 1970s. Those were the times when the federal government dispensed post-sputnik money, with seemingly no strings attached, and the hardware salesmen, like camp followers on payday, swarmed into the building to help the principal spend it and guarantee that no American teacher would be denied the inalienable right to an opaque projector. The paperback book became respectable and contributed mightily to our throwaway society. That score of years is neatly tucked away in Miss Brook's memory book.

It's beginning to be clear that many of the gains of that period will soon be lost. There will be no more smorgasbord of electives to divert the college-bound (too extravagant for the cost-conscious accountants). No more social promotion to bewilder the verbally halt and lame (society can't absorb them, so they might as well do their time in school). Can you read the handwriting (Palmer method) on the wall? The focus is getting clearer: "If you teach English, you teach only reading, grammar, composition." And don't confuse reading with literature, because literature is taught in another department, the humanities.

The teacher who has opted to teach literature in the humanities department will face auditorium-size classes (100–200) with university-like lectures to prepare, while all about the walls allied visuals are projected. When Thoreau deplores the lives of quiet desperation, the walls will bloom with the flora of Walden as well as shots of contrasting places taken from the frenetic lives of the students' own contemporaries. The comfortable teaching of essays all at once, followed by poetry, and then in turn the other four types of literature will have been completely abandoned, as will the course arrangement by prominent authors. Tomorrow's children, like today's, will have a great need to see a pattern to their lives, to find meanings in what they do. Psychological themes will generally be the vehicle for literature within the conglomerate of humanities.

Yes, conglomerates will have come to universal education at last! Music, art, history, and literature are natural shipmates in a sea of Machine Shop, Business Math, Marketing, and Understanding Real Estate. The subjects that humanize us, temper the beast in us, work wonderously well together when taught by a specialist from each field. But since

Francis Bacon's retirement, there are few people sufficiently well rounded to carry it off alone. And don't forget the professional administrator, sniveling over there in the dark, playing with his Texas Instrument. He's just punched out proof that it is cheaper to have one teacher handle a humanities course rather than four. There will be one! To be sure. One teacher exceedingly well prepared in history can gain our sympathy for being uneasy with the fields of art, music, and literature, but cannot be forgiven for seeing John Milton only as Cromwell's secretary and a Puritan political pamphleteer. But the humanities will surely flourish with the funds the government provides through the National Endowments for the Arts and the Humanities. And they can't get along without literature, so lit will have to leave English, and English will revert to what it was in the nineteenth century—composition, grammar, and reading skills.

When the breakup of English departments as we now know them comes about, senior teachers will probably be invited to make a choice. Those who agree to do the read-comp bit can expect smaller classes (fifteen), a smaller load (four), and probably some kind of merit pay. Society by then will be willing to pay any price to get literate citizens, if not literary ones.

That getting will involve the electronic classroom in full flower (or full shock!). Some of its by-products will be blessings, and some will be curses. It may be too soon to decide which is which but not too soon to contemplate. Absentees in the reading class will be able to continue to learn unfamiliar language by punching in a word on a home Touch-Tone® telephone, along with the teacher's ID number, to hear a computer tape prepared earlier give out pronunciations and definitions. The sick students will be able to switch to the teacher on their bedroom television receivers, which have closed-circuit channels to the classroom. Because these are two-way, they will be able to participate in class discussion as the spirit moves them.

By the same means, home-bound students will be able to flash onto their television screen what is called a "dedicated" newspaper or magazine. The teacher will have assembled items from national and local periodicals and television programs she/he wants them to see. Teacher, of course, will be able to use the same principle to display an array of teaching materials for sale by publishers and media firms in order to shop from the comfort of the classroom desk.

Although some schools will still require physical presence in class, most will permit electronic attendance to suffice. Schools, one can be certain, will be the last to give up all attendance requirements, in keeping with the conservative image they have always maintained. But many commercial offices will have led the way by allowing stenographers and bookkeepers to do their work at home with the use of picture-phone hookups. The practice will eventually spread, from co-op students and handicapped students, to all absentees. The extension to Universal Absence is only a short hop in the long history of education.

This same electronic classroom will let the teacher's aide feed in objective tests and scores and then permit an interested parent to call the computer by using the student's secret ID number to learn the child's grades, either cumulative or on a specific exam. Whatever teachers of today may think of the projected electronic classroom, no one can deny that it will be a fund of convenient and instantaneous information.

Union settlements, if not instantaneous, will at least be faster and less acrimonious, because computers will weigh and report out the advantages and disadvantages of bargaining proposals. Everyone will be unionized, of course, including the students and the parents. Although most of the grades a teacher puts in will be objective, she/he may well be permitted to inject "the personal factor," probably limited to 10 percent, determined during contract negotiations.

That contract will serve also to protect the literature teacher from the usual censorship attacks. Gone will be today's familiar heated interest in imagined or real insults to religion, patriotism, or race, probably because Arthur C. Clarke was right in *2001* that we will have come to worship our machines; interstellar contacts will eliminate provincial jingoism; and the black and white races will have fused into a lovely *café au lait.* Everyone will study freely *The Last Temptation of Christ, Slaughterhouse Five,* and *Native Son,* although some may confuse the characters. But in the forbidden places on the no-no list will be prohibition against sexism (no more *Tom Jones, Ginger Man,* Mark Twain, or John Tunis—who was Norman Mailer?). Or prohibition against destruction of the environment (sorry, Frost, about your swinging on birches—who was Hemingway?) . It may sound like more than one can bear, but teachers have played successfully a waiting game all though the years for angers to subside over *Leaves of Grass* or *Grapes of Wrath* or *Nana* or *Ghosts.* Or they have sneaked them in when the censor was off on some other witch hunt. In the future, the titles used will be part of the contract, changed at intervals as fashions change.

The fashion in temporary relationships that the students espouse will make interesting talk in the faculty dining room, over a glass of Blue Nun. As teachers observe these life-styles, it will be obvious that the literature selected will not dismay parents or students. The Pill, vended at coffee machines near the unisex washrooms (with a government warning about health hazards), will have replaced completely the insecurity of close encounters of the forth (*sic*) kind. So one need not hesitate to teach again such classics as *Looking for Mr. Goodbar* or the more recent, sensitive, and popular *Tatum O'Neal Looks Back.*

Whatever changes evolve or revolve, there will be, as there always has been, a sufficient number of older English teachers to keep the optimistic, idealistic young ones informed that teaching was much better in the old days. But most teachers will adjust to changes gracefully and greet the brave new world with hope and inspiration. And they will work hard to reach the modicum of students who find their present dreadfully dull and can barely wait to withdraw a film cassette from the library and go home to watch *2001.*

So what else is new?

Yesterday, Today, and Tomorrow! A Reexamination of Some Nineteenth Century Assumptions

M. ROBERT GRAHAM

Michigan has never really had a present moment. It has a mysterious past and an uncalculable future, attractive and terrifying by turns, but the moment where the two meet is always a time of transition. The state is caught between yesterday and tomorrow, existing less for itself than for what it leads to; it is a road whose ends are distorted by imagination and imperfect knowledge. The great American feeling of being en route—to the unknown, to something new, to the fantastic reality that must lie beyond the mists—is perfectly represented here.

—Bruce Catton
Michigan, 1976

THE MYSTERIOUS PAST

One of my yesterdays, the day I finished the eighth grade in the spring of 1941, was a bench mark that was celebrated with a diploma and pomp and circumstance. Of my several graduations, it is the one that I remember most favorably. Even then, the ceremony was a relic of the past. It was a reminder of the days when a grammar school education was an unusual accomplishment. In the not too distant past of 1900, only seven of every one hundred students in the fifth grade graduated from high school. And as recently as 1932, only thirty of every one hundred who entered school made it through twelfth grade.

On that graduation day, I looked forward with eagerness and some fear in anticipation of Latin, Shakespeare, world history, and algebra in high school. "Puer" and "puella" had become part of my vocabulary as early as the fourth grade. There had been oral readings of *Tom Sawyer, Huckleberry Finn,* and "Paul Revere's Ride." To be forewarned was to be forearmed.

The future of Latin, literature, history, and math proved to be a time of memorization: word lists, conjugations, declensions, ". . . The quality of mercy is not strain'd . . ," assumptions, definitions, conjectures, theorems, and correlates. There was anxiety about today's lesson and tomorrow's test, but in time the world of school came to be my world also. Its assumptions became my assumptions, its definitions, my definitions, and its biases, my biases.

That part of my past has not been a conscious part of my internal dialogue for some time now; but a project for the Oakland County, Michigan, English Advisory Committee and a booklet, *Some Promising Programs in English,* brought the past into contrast with the present. While devising the table of contents, I found myself summarizing the programs into categories: *Communication Skills, Reading, Innovative Programs,* and *Classroom Management.* The programs had names like Project Involve, LAP, CATS, HIT, and Media Now. The descriptions used now-familiar but once foreign terms: ESEA Title I, Title III, start-up costs, funding per student, and "Fifty-two percent gained 1.5 years or greater."

One course, *Creative Life Management,* began its description with a rewriting of a familiar line, "The examined life is the life worth living"—Plato. For me nothing could have been more culturally contrastive: "Life Management" and the "examined life." A personal dialogue of past, present, and future sprang fully armed into my consciousness.

It was at this time that Steve Judy suggested that I might like to contribute to this book. Steve himself had once commented on the growth of English as a school subject. In summarizing that development he concluded that in ". . . 1850 English was a minor subject in the secondary school curriculum, and composition, when taught, usually consisted of monthly or bimonthly essays written on abstract or philosophical subjects with little or no formal instruction. . . . By 1890, however, English had become established as one of the major constituents in the high school curriculum; composition was perhaps the most widely discussed school subject; and composition teaching had assumed a shape that has been largely unchanged up to the present." [1]

In the fifty years between 1850 and 1900 some twenty million immigrants were admitted to the United States. This influx created a cultural-linguistic battleground. The diverse cultures and languages were a threat to the virtually homogeneous Anglo-American society, and this threat contributed to the growth of English as a school subject.

Gene L. Piché describes the 1865 "gut level linguistic fear" which led, in 1894, to the NEA Committee of Ten's formulation of English as three parts literature and one part composition.[2] This formulation was

[1] Judy, Stephen, "The Teaching of English Composition in American Schools," unpublished doctoral dissertation, Northwestern University, 1967.

[2] Piché, Gene L., "Class Culture in the Development of the High School English Curriculum, 1880–1900," *Research in Teaching English,* vol. II, Spring, 1977, p. 20.

to provide moral value, civil order, and social cement for a diverse society. It would provide linguistic insignia of class and status, as well as
vocational skills for an industrial society.

The assumptions behind the Committee of Ten's formulation
were, in essence,

- that the schools should provide the means to one language, one
  culture, one ethnicity for all;
- that the schools have a responsibility to teach a formal standard
  usage that would serve as a badge of social class and ethnic
  heritage;
- that the schools have a responsibility to maintain civil and industrial order by inculcating a single set of moral values and
  developing students' vocational skills.

James Squire [3] in 1966 attested to the influence of these assumptions on the high school curriculum. Literature and composition were
still at a three-to-one ratio, and composition was taught by "after the
act" correction procedures.

As recently as September 1977, Candida Gillis described a similar English classroom:

> If you are a student in an English class taught by a
> mythical "average" respondent [to this survey of classroom prac-
> tices], you are in a senior high school class with students with
> above average or mixed abilities. Your class stresses literature and
> writing. You write exposition, narratives of personal experience,
> and interpretations and analyses of literature. You read many
> short stories and novels, and your text is an anthology. You
> spend time in class talking freely about the literature, discussing
> study guide questions, and writing. If you enrolled in the course
> wanting to make movies, write scripts or advertisements, read
> off-beat, technical, or minority literature, take field trips, or
> study transformational grammar or features of dialects, you are
> out of luck.[4]

The English formulation of 1894, the one I took without question
as my own, and the English classroom of 1977 were largely the same. The
content has been tinkered with, but not the substance. Similarly two of
my English teachers in the early 1940s, Miss Brown and Miss Miller

---

[3] Squire, James R., "National Study of High School English Programs: A
School for All Seasons," *The English Journal*, vol. 55, March 1966, p. 282.

[4] Gillis, Candida, "The English Classroom 1977: A Report on the EJ Reader-
ship Survey," *The English Journal*, vol. 66, September 1977, p. 20.

from South Hills High, who seemed in hindsight such humanistic innovators, really weren't innovators, just good teachers of the Anglo tradition. In 1894, English, motivated by "gut level" fear and guided by college-oriented decision makers, had turned its head upward and placed its hand upon the ladder of success, an act reminiscent of those lines which have been recited in English 2B ever since:

> ". . . lowliness is young ambition's ladder,
> Whereto the climber-upward turns his face;
> But when he once attains the upmost round,
> He then unto the ladder turns his back,
> Looks in the clouds, scorning the base degrees
> By which he did ascend: . . ." [5]

In aspiring to a secure place in the high school curriculum, the English education equivalents of 1894 favored the study of the structure of English over thought. Philology, literary criticism, and scientific language study became the curriculum; thinking was to come later, in college. By condemning the existing practice of offering more than one course in English—college bound, technical or scientific, and terminal— the committee, by implication, recommended that all students subscribe to a curriculum dominated by college entrance requirements. In addition, in recommending a four-year English curriculum in high school, the committee emphasized the importance of English as a discipline among disciplines, rather than as a process. Those students who didn't fit the rigors of study in the discipline were subsequently rejected.

The issue was not settled then. The James Hosic Committee on the Reorganization of Secondary School English reacted strongly against college domination in 1917, and twenty years later, W. Wilbur Hatfield chaired the debate that led to the NCTE Experience Curriculum of 1935. Even today, *eighty years* after the formulations of the Committee of Ten were published, proponents of educational assessment, vocational education, and the many other sources of dissent are voicing dissatisfaction with educators' scorn of the "base" elements of the school population. Albert Bandura calls this interaction between English and society "reciprocal determinism." [6] As one acts, the environment is changed, which, in turn, affects the actor. There is an altered environment about us today.

---

[5] Shakespeare, William, "The Tragedy of Julius Caesar," Act II, Scene I, in *The Riverside Shakespeare*, vol. II, edited by G. B. Evans, Houghton Mifflin Co., Boston, 1974, p. 1111.

[6] Bandura, Albert, *Social Learning Theory*, Prentice-Hall, Englewood Cliffs, N.J., 1976.

For example, back in that mysterious past again, back in the environment of my elementary school days, there was a testy sort of neighborhood pluralism. By religion there were Catholics, Protestants, and Jews. The Catholics went to one school and the Protestants and Jews to another. The buildings were located at opposite ends of the neighborhood. The respective religions were made physically prominent by buildings positioned along the main boulevard. As I passsed an unfamiliar structure, I felt a sense of curiosity about the interior, the "curriculum" or ceremony. There was a sense of separate and equal (if not of equal goodness).

Within my own school there was another sort of pluralism. In my class there were Irish, Italians, Germans, and Syrians, all united by religion: Catholicism. In the classroom we competed for academic position made physical by the seating arrangement. Seven rows of seven seats were anchored on the oak floor. First row, first seat, left was top student; last row, last seat, right was the bottom. The warmers of those last few seats were older and larger. The school community took care of them until they reached sixteen, when, I imagine, they traded their school custodial positions for low-paying outside jobs. They were the first and most obvious of the "base" elements.

We were a brotherhood of religion and school among others. But in the classroom and in our living patterns, we lived friendly but separate existences. The Irish lived at the top of the hill, the Italians down the hill East, the Germans across the hill North. Milton Gordon describes these subcultures in his *Assimilation in American Life,* using the term "cultural pluralism." [7] The school bound us into a brotherhood against the others, but within the classroom we led friendly, parallel, but not integrated, lives. We were "a limited, structurally pluralistic subsociety," to use sociological jargon.

In South Hills High School, my elementary class joined those of several other elementary schools. Jews, Catholics, Protestants, the ethnic groups—and now Blacks—were together in parallel, culturally pluralistic conditions. We took on new labels of College, Business, and General but with one English curriculum for all. After a year or so there were disappearances: some went to vocational school, some dropped out, and my classes were made up more and more of the same competitors. Perhaps half of us finished high school. English class was the great separator.

In this way, my high school was pluralistic. Each of us belonged to groups, and there was some intragroup exchange of opinion and

---

[7] Gordon, Milton, *Assimilation in American Life,* Oxford University Press, New York, 1964.

friendship and athletic brotherhood; but the groups—religious, ethnic, racial, and academic—were *not* equal. The rewards to some were greater than those to others, and the school didn't really have but one "own" to take care of: those who succeeded under the existing curriculum.

In reality, the nineteenth century "gut level linguistic fear" had actually perpetuated the structural pluralism that existed at the time of immigration. English, which, according to the curriculum planners, was to cement society, was, in fact, used to exclude. Standard English became the mark of "in-ness." Eighty years later, the conflict promoted by the exclusionary school practices of which standard English was a symptom now threatens to fracture society, not cement it. The "actor" is now acted upon.

BETWEEN YESTERDAY AND TOMORROW

If this is where we've been, what about Bruce Catton's, ". . . feeling of being *en route*—to the unknown, to something new. . . ." Is there an English classroom lying "beyond the mists—"?

To answer this I'd like to make some assumptions of my own. To begin with, I'll assume that by looking at decision makers we can glean some picture of their decisions.

Applebee [8] gives credit to both the 1894 National Conference on Uniform Entrance Requirements in English (it argued for compulsory English study) and the Committee of Ten (it unified the subject and gave it prestige) for winning recognition for English studies. The Committee of Ten was college-dominated: five college presidents, one college professor, the Commissioner of Education, and three high school leaders. The English Conference of the committee was composed of seven college people, one superintendent, and two high school leaders. The National Conference on Uniform Entrance Requirements in English was concerned with standardizing high school curricula so that a college could count on the training a high school graduate received and the quality of his grades. Our college-oriented curriculum is the result of their decisions: standard English for immigrants and migrants, or out; college-prep skills for the favored.

Who makes the decisions today? One recent decision maker has been the law. Chester Nolte points out in the May 1976 *American School Board Journal* that law and politics have entered public education

---

[8] Applebee, Arthur N., *Tradition and Reform in the Teaching of English: A History*, National Council of Teachers of English, Urbana, Illinois, 1974, p. 38.

through the courts as much because of inactive school people as because of the contesting parties.[9]

It was the Supreme Court that recognized discrimination in 1954 and Congress that passed the 1964 Civil Rights Act. Since then we have been influenced by Title I, Compensatory Education (84 percent of all elementary schools receive some money); Title IV-B, Guidance and Library materials, low-economic limited-English speakers; Title IV-C, Bilingual Demonstration; Title VII, Bilingual Grants; and Title IX, Equal Rights for Women. In addition, other legislation has influenced vocational, career, bilingual, and special education. Money given to further these ends requires that the recipients design a program according to strict guidelines, develop an advisory committee made up of at least 51 percent of those served by the grant, and submit to strict evaluation procedures. Leadership comes from state and federal educational bureaucracies guided by court guidelines.

Faced with increased pressure to alter programs to meet legal ends, local districts also have been restricted by a reduction or stoppage of general aid from state coffers by a formula seeking to equalize the economic basis of education. This has come about through court guidance (in California, for example) and voter pressure. Inflation, which raises tax bases beyond equalization levels, also contributes.

If the courts and politics serve as the motivating "morality" to educational change, then who influences legislative action? The UAW, the Urban League, LaRaza, teacher unions, the major city governments, and other interest blocks are all represented in the state capitols and seek to influence decisions.

There are three more assumptions to be explored as we look toward the future of education:

First, I assume that these decision makers are in the process of identifying someplace "good" for English to go, and that necessarily, and in due time, "good place" will be defined.

Second, I assume that joint political efforts using the carrot/stick technique will produce movement toward that "good place."

And finally, I assume that that place will be different from the one we now aspire to in the classroom. Where the old classroom was teacher dependent, the new will be more program dependent. Where good instruction once depended on good, motivated teachers, it will now come to depend more on good program objectives, procedures, and cooperation.

---

[9] Nolte, Chester, "How to Survive the Supreme Court's Momentous New Strictures on School People," *American School Board Journal*, vol. II, May 1975, p. 162.

The "good place," then, for English will be defined in legislation, in Department of Education rules, regulations, and guidelines, and at the bargaining table in arbitrated curriculum sessions. At present, the definitions of the good place look remarkably like those described by Gillis, Squire, and Applebee (and, with trappings removed, like "the good place" of the nineteenth century).

As the courts point, as the legislature implements, as the bureaucracy promulgates, and as teachers and boards of education arbitrate, two big questions arise: Is it possible that we can find ways of working together to decrease educational inequality? Is it possible that, as we work on the English curriculum, some of the details we come to agree on will be meaningful ones based in the rapidly growing body of knowledge about language growth and acquisition? The concern must be with both the process by which we do things and the results of that process.

Let me give an example of how complex specific learning problems can be from my personal experience with bilingual education. Michigan Law PL 294 (Bilingual Education) was the result of two forces: The federal government was threatening to impose standards, and Michigan Latino groups were pressuring their legislators and others for equal opportunity in the schools. The law required a bilingual program in any school district with twenty or more students in a language classification. The classroom models implied were ones based on experience in the Southwest.

What turned up in Oakland County and other sections of Michigan were multiple language groups in many schools: Forty-two languages were found in Oakland County, seventy-three in Detroit. Not only were many langauge groups found, but there were specific definitional problems within a language classification. Many students who came to this country directly from Iraq, South America, or Taiwan, say, with no English or English as a foreign language were found after a time to be successfully competing in the schools, while students from the same language and cultural background who were born here did not do as well. This has led Renato Gonzalez, Director of Michigan Bilingual Education, to speculate on some of the language variables related to a successful integration in Michigan classrooms. He has noted that some children come to school with their native non-English language intact. They may or may not have had academic training in their cultural background. Other children reach school caught, in a sense, between two languages. For example, a child from an Italian background may come speaking his dialect so spiced with English words and pronunciation borrowings that he would be unintelligible in his parents' native province. Still another child arrives in kindergarten a monospeaker of English but using his parents' French intonation and pronunciation. Each of these children poses different instructional problems.

Thus, the legislation brought about a response from the schools, and the response was more complex than anyone had imagined. The carrot and stick combined to identify a wide range of issues and problems that had previously been ignored by the schools.

It seems apparent to me that there is a new motivation evident in the latter part of the twentieth century. The decision makers may have been educated in classrooms little different from nineteenth-century ones, and they may think in many ways like nineteenth-century leaders, but they are not the same people who made those earlier decisions. The environment is forcing change, and inevitably the English curriculum of the future will be decidedly different from that of yesterday and today. Its details will need to be more accessible to measurement and arbitration. At first, as is now done, there will be a tendency to grab at the more easily measured details and to measure too many of them. Eventually, larger growth steps or bench marks will be selected. Growth patterns will become discernible, and individual differences and problems will be documented. It will be possible to relate activities and materials to growth success.

The day will come when programs in all subject areas will be founded on the best principles of learning theory and on understanding how people learn through language. We will not find thirty students in a class taking the same exam at the same time. Norm-referenced testing will disappear. Testing will be specific to the program. Because of the complexity, programs will be more routine from classroom to classroom. Schools will be more dependent on those programs and less on teacher uniqueness.

Those people who hold to the old assumptions of one language, one culture, one ethnicity, and formal standard usage as a badge of social class and ethnic heritage will be in for a difficult period of adjustment. If we are to bring these visions to reality, the question to ask now is, "What will we become as the environment changes and acts upon us and the new generation? How will we reciprocate?" What I fear most is that the decision makers will not be able to "associate together" and nothing will be done. Tocqueville pointed out about American society in the 1830s, "Among the laws which rule human societies there is one which seems to be more precise and clear than others. If men are to remain civilized, or to become so, the art of associating together must grow and improve in the same ratio in which the quality of conditions is increased." [10]

---

[10] Tocqueville, Alexis de, *Democracy in America*, vol. 2, Harper & Row, New York, 1966, p. 116.

Who Aims at the Middle ...

STANLEY COOK

"Who aims at the middle misses both ends." Certainly this aphorism applies to the classroom, where heterogeneity is generally the rule. For instance, grouping by chronological age, by ability, or by elective programs geared to thematic interests achieves one sort of homogeneity at the expense of others. An extreme way of handling student diversity has been to reduce the curriculum to such common denominators as rote learning, or the mystical goals of *mastery* and *coverage*. Another extreme makes no pretense to conformity, but is, rather, the completely permissive program of allowing each individual to find his own goals in his own way.

In no other school subject are the dilemmas imposed by student diversity so complex as they are in the field of English, itself a multiform discipline. As a consequence, English teachers have always sought for some magic curriculum, some single course design, or some textbook—some gimmick or other—that will answer everybody's needs and that will not require a combination of saint and genius to use it.

Nominations for this panacea, this utopian complete answer, have been legion. The profession has learned much from them, and as a result, it is likely that the best all-time teachers of English are now at work. Such men and women have not fixed on some formula, accepting all its limitations and remaining blind to its defects. He or she may have a personal, even a unique, style, but he selects the best brush and the best color, and she the best device and the best material for the task at hand, and not for always. The great teacher is an artist, not a technician.

Without slighting the enthusiastic neophyte, one may usually expect the master teacher to have several years' experience. This experience has confirmed what the college professors have told him—both the idealists and the witty iconoclasts. Having read the books of protest, he has been amused or exasperated to find how many of the examples, futile or stupid, may be found in his own school environment. He has searched among more positive writings for tools appropriate to his own needs and his own skills. He has tested the old and sampled the new, and although realistic in his concern for the basics of the three Rs, he knows that they are not enough. He has learned, too, that love is not enough, and that dissent does not get the job done.

From his failures, both traditional and experimental, he has learned how much to expect. Last year's adventures in puppetry do not impress this year's ninth graders, and he is no longer so enamored of a morning's success as to allow it to become the afternoon's fiasco. Remembering how ardently his classes resisted Holmes and Lowell, he is not too dismayed by less than total involvement in the dramatization of scenes from *Huckleberry Finn*. Nor does he easily forget the 30 percent median score on that quiz covering his finest lecture, the one on "Transcendentalism."

The experienced teacher has become aware that there is very little that is new under the sun. *The English Journal* tells him what is being tried and retried, and Silberman, Holt, and Kozol have not made him forget the constructive influences of Dora Smith and Ralph Tyler, of the *Experience Curriculum* and the Eight-Year Study. In effect, he knows that few, if any, of today's experimental modes have sprung full blown on the American educational scene.

A major concept of progressive education is taking the child where he is. But the child is not a discrete entity, to be tutored alone as was John Stuart Mill. His classmates, his school, and his community form a matrix that must also be taken where it is. The wisest reforms are the ones that are possible. Consequently, the experienced teacher must know more than the printed history of education; he is familiar with educational trends in the district where he works and with the prevailing wind conditions. In his school, for instance, the coeducational course on personality development, including sex education, drew a dozen sections in 1955. Today, restored to the Home Economics Department, it attracts one hundred girls. Core courses were discontinued in the junior high schools when the dynamic teachers who made them go became guidance counselors. He knows, however, of the two elementary schools with viable open classrooms.

His professional environment includes community attitudes as well as the written and the latent rules. He knows who are the legitimate critics, who are the cranks and the crackpots, and who of each group is to be heeded or to be discreetly ignored. He has measured his principal and his department head, and he is aware of the criteria by which he and his classes are to be evaluated. Accordingly, he can judge when to inch his way, and when to go all out; when to tack, and when to run with the wind.

There are pertinent socioeconomic and family patterns to know about. Ralph Tyler reports two schools in Lincoln, Nebraska, with what they called "open" classrooms. One of them was a

. . . parochial school in an area of working-class people, mostly second-generation Irish and German. Their homes were pretty rigid, but the open classroom, conducted by nuns, was highly creative. The kids thrived in it; it gave them a sense of freedom that contrasted with the more restricted environment outside. Then I visited an open classroom in the poorest part of town. The children were mostly blacks and Mexican-Americans from disorganized homes. A great many of the children came from homes where only the mother was present, and she was so distracted that there was very little structure. In the open classroom these kids were just completely lost. They had no sense of direction and nothing to live up to. The open classroom for these children seemed to me to be a great mistake.[1]

This instance is quoted not for the example of the open classroom but to suggest that circumstances alter cases, and that one had better know what the circumstances are. The wise teacher learns, as Tyler goes on to say, that there is no use in an educator's saying, "We must have an innovation," until he has identified a problem and measured the situation.

The "problem" that requires innovative treatment sometimes lies less in the home than in the school, less in the children sent to school than in what the school has made of them. The realization does not come overnight, but the alert teacher soon becomes aware of the kinds of discipline within which and against which he and his classes operate. He discovers their capacities for independent and small-group procedures, their skills in making decisions, and their complete trust or their practiced skepticism when he asks, "What do *you* think?" He finds out whether their creative experiences have been limited to scissors-and-paste collages, or whether they have included writing limericks or letters to Japan. Such elements are among those he must consider in choosing the best alternatives to serve the needs of Joe and Tom and Irene, second hour, Room 221.

There are others. Since thirty kids in a room built to house thirty-six may accomplish many things that a smaller class packed wall to wall cannot do, the teacher has checked out the available alternatives in space. He knows by what cajolery or reciprocation he can shift his class to the stage, to a corner of an empty auditorium, or to an unused storeroom, and for which days or for which weeks. He knows how many

---

[1] "An Interview with Ralph Tyler," *Phi Delta Kappan*, vol. LVIII, March, 1977, p. 546.

kids he may send out of his classroom, and where and for how long. He knows, too, the rules and the facilities for taking a class, or part of it, from the building.

Not all the physical factors are architectural. Other resources are to be reckoned with, resources that can make this project or wreck that one. Obviously, there are textbooks and supplements, reference works, and school and room libraries. A school that is lean in one area may be rich in another. It takes time to learn which is which, and to what extent the public library is suitably complementary. The good teacher does not depend on the kids' reports; he checks personally when either library is available, for how many people, and under what circumstances, and whether either is maintained essentially for use or as a reliquary. Uncommitted funds may be available for books or films or recordings; he knows who holds them. He has sought out free books and films from state and regional collections.

After a few years in school, a teacher has learned to get on with his superiors and his fellow English teachers, and he has learned on whom he can count for concrete suggestions or for moral support. He knows what kind of cooperation he may expect from which art or music or typing teacher. This librarian will help prepare a list of novels about the immigrant in America. That custodian will tolerate rearrangement or disarrangement of classroom furniture. To have good relations with one's staff seems too obvious a matter to mention, but the point is that some will be very helpful, and others will be resolutely resentful of any deviation from the orthodox. The former are the innovator's allies; the latter he circumvents.

Perhaps he has met and befriended—outside of school—a reporter, an advertising man, a sculptress, a book collector, a cellist, a poet. And from such a reservoir of local talent, he has on occasion tapped the services of a Lebanese physician to tell his students of the role of poetry in the Arabic-speaking world, or an architect who has brought his own slides to make more meaningful a humanistic approach to the baroque in literature.

Experience brings self-knowledge. The teacher has learned his own levels of annoyance, such as how much noise he can tolerate in a laboratory writing situation, or the degree to which he can put up with the complaints of colleagues who object to his kids' being vocally excited about anything whatever. He knows more than he did about his own biases—political, racial, sexual, or aesthetic—and the ways in which these biases intrude on his judgments of student work. He knows that he can never become a replica of Mark Hopkins, or Miss Dove, or A. S. Neill. Like his students, he is unique, and his best self is his own.

Nor does he judge his students solely by a common graduated scale. Student performance is gauged not only by traditional measures of reading and writing but also by how far an informal situation has brought Mary Alice out of her role as a perennial recluse, or whether Jerry has quit skipping English, or whether Lennie no longer submits blank papers. He balances Anthea's thirty books read in a semester of free-reading opportunities against Arthur's three-fourths of a page written on Lindbergh's *We,* a paper which got his brother through high school and which has been his sole contribution to every English class since seventh grade.

The English teacher has progressed beyond his own sophomoric beginnings. He now suspects how much he does not know. An NCTE President back in the 1930s, Rollo LaVerne Lyman, once said that the best English teacher is one who knows the most about everything else. Narrowly, the comment applies to the observation that the good critic has one foot in the text and the other in the world, but Lyman was concerned with more than literary ivory towers. The broader application has meaning for any teacher who presumes to guide thirty students with thirty different backgrounds to their assorted goals in independent study, or in core commitments, or in an open classroom. He becomes acutely aware that he has much to learn about such matters as three-dimensional photography, black dialects, and Sicilian folklore.

He has, of course, done some reading, a truly incredible amount of every variety, and he is still reading, or at least skimming materials that have adolescent appeals and values. He has not forsaken Shakespeare and Twain and Chekhov, but he has added, not only from the classics of three thousand years and a dozen countries, but also from the contemporary and the popular. He can lead a student hooked on science fiction to such great utopias and dystopias as *Fahrenheit 451, Looking Backward,* and *R.U.R.* He knows that literature of protest is not an invention of the 1960s or 1970s, and he can prove it by introducing Swift and Voltaire, Galsworthy and Gorky. Or, conversely, he can move from the past to Steinbeck, Orwell, Vonnegut, and a hundred others. Regardless of his students' complexions, he reads and recommends Langston Hughes and Ralph Ellison. His knowledge of women in literature does not begin with *Pride and Prejudice* and end with *Jane Eyre.*

And so on. And so on. Yet, although he is omnivorous and insatiable, he is not indiscriminate. He may not like Dickens or Hesse or McKuen, but he knows them.

Lyman's "everything else" includes more than literature, a great deal more. Having taught for four years or ten or twenty-five does not make the teacher omniscient. He has learned, however, to help a student to find, use, and understand local sources of information about whatever esoteric subjects may inspire intensive reading and writing. For him, it is not enough to smile vacuously and murmur, "That's fine, honey; keep it coming." On his own, he investigates at least enough to be able to ask

leading questions, and he trains his students to use appropriate research techniques in local museums and libraries and in courteous and skillful interviews with convenient authorities, in school and out. What expertise the teacher *does* have he is willing to swap with a fellow instructor. He has, on occasion, exchanged his guitar and his singing of American folk ballads with the teacher down the hall, who can give his kids a word about making home movies.

One lifetime is not enough to accumulate all the needed lore, but although, as Ken Donelson has pointed out,[2] the task is an impossible one, the experienced teacher has at least begun on it. Seeing the insufficiency of customary forms, he has not waited for a federal grant to do something, nor has he waited for *the total answer* in which he can invest his everything. Believing that in education, as in industry, pilot runs precede full production, he has sampled the possibilities. He may have taught the text three days a week and turned the kids loose the other two. Having succeeded with free reading one week per month, he is prepared to set up a semester elective in "Explorations in Reading." Having brought along five students in independent study, he is confident in directing twenty-five, and he may ask for time to do so. Having found benefits in pupil–teacher planning, he may have moved on to some of the techniques of the core curriculum within the limits of his forty-eight minute class period, and he is now ready, should he wish, to ask for half a day in an open classroom.

He may not make any of these requests, at least not at this time, but he has tried the old, the not-so-old, and the new, and he understands the options. This is his freedom, to choose among tested alternatives. Absolute freedom is, of course, a myth. Neither student nor teacher ever has it, but the more each knows, the more choices he has, and perhaps that is what education is all about.

If, since there are so many more veteran teachers than novices, their successes are varied and visible, so unfortunately are their mishaps and their mediocrities. There are some who do not read and who have not had one new idea since 1942. Others, who began well, have become perfunctory cynics and the prima donnas of their departments.

So it is also with beginners, some of whom are amazingly successful. After all, the novice has the appeal of belonging to the students' generation, an unspoiled liking for kids, the confidence and energy of youth, and some relatively uncommitted time. Idealist and activist, he resents lockstep programs of every sort, and especially the slow pace by

---

[2] Donelson, Ken, "Some Responsibilities for English Teachers Who Already Face an Impossible Job," *The English Journal,* vol. 66, September 1977, pp. 27–32.

which change comes about. Education courses have confirmed his inclinations, and, diploma in hand, he is off and running.

So far, so good.

He brings not only his enthusiasm but also an awareness of what is succeeding elsewhere, plus a willingness to learn and a willingness to try. Uncommitted to a filing cabinet filled with set plans and quizzes, he investigates the kids as well as the course of study, and introduces patterns derived from the situation instead of from established habit. What he does is contagious. Some of his verve reignites the passion of peers whose fires have burned low, and he recalls to them not only their earlier goals but also past successes that may be resurrected. As Goethe says, "That which is new is only the old, forgotten." Thus, he converts his own classroom and others as well into viable educational experiences.

Not every novice is so apt.

Let's suppose for a moment that one is told, in effect, "We hired you as a good prospective teacher. So go and do your thing." Whether he is told as much, or whether he takes it upon himself, he makes certain choices, anywhere from teaching as he was taught, to the Socratic method, to a wide-open classroom. Instead of taking the kids where they are, he has in advance fixed upon his Grand Variant, which he cannot wait to impose on his classes, whatever their peculiar interests or needs. His plan may work well, but very likely it is either a wrong course or an untimely one. His class meets on the front lawn to talk about *life,* and he wonders why they wander. He releases them on vague errands from which they return empty-handed. They spend a semester vainly attempting to find out what he *really* wants of them. The more he tries to reach them, the more he fails; the more he fails, the harder he tries, until one of two things happens. He forsakes teaching, or he reverts to some authoritarian pattern perhaps even more stringent than the one he thought he was rebelling against. In either case, he is lost to *the cause* that drew him into teaching.

Paradoxically, if his grand experiment succeeds, he may reach the same end. A design that is patently wrong for his first teaching assignment may go very well for a time on the strength of his personal appeal and enthusiasm. Confirmed in his choice, he makes it his canon, avoiding any heresies of adaptation to the here, the now, or the whom. The time comes when diligence, sincerity, and personality no longer suffice, and in his disillusionment he blames the kids and comes to the same decision he might have made had his failure been immediate.

The lesson for both the beginner and the veteran, then, is expecting too much and, knowing too little, having too few options. And how much knowledge is enough? There is never enough. But the teacher, whatever his age, knows that he is on his way when

- *Both he and his students have choices.*

- *His focus has shifted from the median to the range to the individual.*

- *He is reaching the quick and the slow and the docile and the reluctant.*

- *He listens more than he declaims.*

- *The kids are learning reading and writing as well as "everything else."*

- *They think instead of being thought for.*

- *Discipline grows out of the project at hand instead of some Procrustean Code.*

- *Learning continues when he leaves the room.*

- *The classroom walls are not fixed.*

- *He no longer feels guilty about substituting Gwendolyn Brooks for William Cullen Bryant.*

- *Excited kids outnumber the grade-hounds who stop by after the dismissal bell.*

- *He shares their excitement.*

- *Fellow teachers are borrowing ideas as well as chalk and dictionaries.*

- *Bells ring too soon.*

Obviously, when these kinds of things happen, he is not doing something right; he is doing *many* things right. He has known the options, and he has chosen well among them. One of the didactic little stories in the *McGuffey Readers* tells of a boy who won an archery contest in the rain because he had more than one string to his bow.

Knowing and selecting is harder work than fetching the perennial plan book out of drawer B. It can be worth it. One of the recurring pleasures of the devoted teacher is getting to know his new students in September and in February. That thrill can be a continuing one when, instead of setting out the mold and announcing, "Conform!" he asks himself—and them—"How best do we proceed from here? There are alternatives."

An Intense Teacher

KEN MACRORIE
WITH JOHN BENNETT

Over the last ten years many high school and college teachers have sent me their students' writing. The papers that stand out for precision and emotional intensity were written almost always by students of one teacher—John Bennett of Central High School, Kalamazoo, Michigan. I have visited his classes and for six years with him published *Unduressed,* a magazine of our students' writing. In mind and heart I carry around with me incidents in the lives of his students. That is how well they were realized on paper. Therefore, this interview with John Bennett. He describes a way and an attitude that I hope will belong to many teachers in the future.

—K.M.

KM: John, how did you get started in teaching?

JB: I was a camp counselor, a lifeguard. I found myself in authority positions, but I remember I didn't know what teaching was. I thought it was the imparting of material or skills. Only after teaching a year or two did I find that that wasn't true at all.

KM: Before we get into your philosophy of teaching, I'd like to ask what you do with thirty kids in a writing class.

JB: Every morning I greet each kid as he comes through the door either by name or by asking some question—an irrelevant question, usually, because it's early in the morning. I do not allow a "class" to exist. I make sure each individual is met as an individual all the way through the course, and I think that everybody knows that a group of thirty kids operates differently from the way the same kids act one-on-one. The key here is to maintain the one-on-one even in a group situation. Another thing is that you have to have your flanks covered emotionally. You have to be satisfied with who you are and enjoy what you're doing—love the kids, like the kids. Otherwise you can't do it.

KM: Satisfied with who you are?

JB: You have to teach yourself, which means you have to like yourself, and then you have to like the kids and then you're going to like

29

each other. And you have to strike with each other's world, even if you're forty or fifty or sixty or seventy, and then the kids will listen to you. You know I don't even play rock music in class anymore? I used to play the music they liked, and now I play the music *I* like—and *some* of what they like. The thing is: access to their psyche, because the biggest problem the kids face is the irrelevancy of their parents, the tenuousness of their self-esteem. They're looking at themselves so intensely, so hard. They're so scared and petrified, and the only adults they really run into— outside of a boss and maybe the minister of the church—are the teachers. And if the teachers do not help build their self-esteem—help them be creative—they're destroyed.

JB: That's a big order, but I don't think it's what society asks.

KM: Society feels that the teacher must teach skills, and they're not aware that the teacher teaches himself. A teacher teaches his perspective, his attitude, his biases. And if he's wise, he doesn't hide behind his material and say, "I'm not a Republican and I'm not a Democrat and therefore I'll teach history objectively." That's dumb. There isn't a student in the classroom who doesn't know who you are within four or five days after you've walked into the room. There just isn't any way that you can lie. If you're in the middle of a divorce action or are an alcoholic, if you are a religious fanatic, these things are picked up.

KM: Other teachers say things like this, only not so perceptively, but they don't end up teaching students any self-discipline or skills.

JB: Teaching is a double-edged sword. It's about 60 percent teaching or evolving your own humanistic viewpoint and about 40 percent skills. You begin with your attitude or view; and after that's established, you can approach them on skills. The thing that bothers me is that the sole reason many teachers exist is to teach a series of skills, which—let's face it—are not that difficult to understand but are not remembered from one year to another. Grammar is taught every single year but never learned. That's because the skill is not tied in with the student's personal existence.

KM: I want to ask what you do to begin your writing class.

JB: We start from their ground, from their being, their perspective. The first thing I ask them to do is write for ten minutes, to put down in pen or pencil whatever thoughts they have in their head at that moment. I know the line, "My mind is a blank," but I point out that a mind is never blank from the minute one is born. I tell them, "Your mind is always pumping out pictures and all you have to do is record them." They write right off the top of their heads, as fast as they can. They ignore grammar, punctuation, spelling. Then I have them write each day. I can do other things during the hour. I can be teaching lit, journalism, drama, even though my emphasis is on writing. But at the first of the hour the kid sits down and writes what he sees to be truth for him at that instant. And so on throughout the year. What I do is simply add to this the discipline of the writer's craft. It's fairly obvious that he will speak in clichés, in colloquialisms, in dialect, with the shortcuts that we all have when we're speaking, but when we come down to writing we have a certain set of rules that an English teacher has when people try to communicate with other people through writing.

KM: Rules?

JB: My rule is that, even on the first day, if we're going to write to other people we must do so with precision and clarity. Anything that blocks that kind of communication leaves room for lies, distortion, and inaccurate problem-solving. So, second day, just free writing. And third day, fourth day, fifth day. Now these are all personal writings. Hand 'em in to me. I don't read them. I just look at 'em. Probably take ten seconds for each paper, fifteen seconds at the most, just to see whether the kid is recording what he perceives to be the truth. I don't put anything on the paper other than my name at the bottom to show that I've read it. I just remove the idea that the teacher is censor, the teacher is judge; I simply emphasize the teacher as watcher, someone looking on. So at the end of the first week I say, "Take one of those four or five writings and type it up as best you can, put it on a ditto carbon, and hand it in to me and put your name on the top sheet of the ditto only so I know that you have the assignment in. The class will not see your name. Ditto enough copies for the class, hand them out, and we'll go through your writing in class as a public business. Then we'll see your writing, not in relation to the secret criteria of John Bennett, who will impart a B over an A on your paper, but in relation to an audience-oriented classroom where the class gets to hear not only my perspective of how well you wrote the truth but whether or not your truths are getting across to the other kids."

KM: That's the first week. Where does that lead?

JB: From these first assignments, I introduce one concept: We've thrown out spelling, we've thrown out punctuation, all the usual things, just to get somebody to write the truth; so the first time I might say something like, "For the next writing, I'd like you to write about one thing." And from that we get to the concept of focus. Next we go to a request that they write about one thing in phrases that they've never seen before in print. Each time you make an assignment like that you allow the kid to put a frame of reference on his reality, his perspective of what truth is for him, and he begins to analyze and see what he sees clearly. After that he begins to understand the difference between lying and truth.

KM: There's that word *truth*. Teachers always ask me about that.

JB: I have three levels of truth. First, *peripheral* truth, which is to say, "I went across the street and bought a quart of milk," and yes, it's the truth, but who cares? Who would want to read about it? It's everyday mundane truth. And then there's the second, *primary* truth, which is, "I fell out of a tree and broke my arm, and felt the blood ooze into the sand." Ninety percent of the writing that writers do is on this level because it's interesting to them—they experienced it. It's also interesting to an audience. And then there's the third level: *gut* truth, which is writing down to the bottom of everything you've ever felt, or known, or believed.

KM: "Writing down to the bottom of everything?"

JB: You're writing down to the very essence of what you ever felt. Now writers just don't get to that level often. They may touch it once in a while. It's when a writer gets down to the core of his existence. So I say to the kids, "I want you to write at the primary level, and you might even strike the gut level. What I don't want you to write about is life on the peripheral level of truth."

KM: And you just scan these? You can tell whether a paper is alive or whether it's written in what I call "Engfish" just by reading a couple of sentences?

JB: Sure. I can pick it up, and bam! I know. You don't treat writing as gold. You treat it as merely an exercise in reality screening, reality perceiving. By the way, you'll have students who can't tell the truth, who can't perceive even their reality accurately. And they will go through the whole year, and lie and lie, and when we pick one of their writings to go public as we do each week, the kids will say, "This is not true!" and the writer will not be able to understand why it's not the truth.

KM: In college writing classes, I sometimes get students who can't write anything but pretentious, pseudo-scholarly stuff. Sometimes they will drop out of class early because this kind of writing doesn't score with me or anyone else in the class.

JB: I don't get that very much in high school, probably because students haven't been trained so long in that kind of writing. The people who cannot tell the truth are so damaged that they cannot look at themselves or their experiences without maintaining a tremendous distance and feeling that the material is more important than their perspective on it. It's not that the Civil War is not important; it's not that the Battle of Appomattox is not important; it's not that women's liberation isn't important; it's that the amount of knowledge a student can bring to bear on any one of those subjects without a tremendous amount of research is negligible. Now, if you're Barbara Tuchman you can sit in the Washington Public Library and you can study for two years and then sit down and write *The Guns of August.* You'll write that material not as some kind of outside discourse on 1914 but as an intimate part of your experience because you've immersed yourself in this research. Well, what happens is that a child—or even an adult—is sent to write on the Republican

Party and has not done his homework, has not done his research, which takes years. And so he cannot tell the truth. He literally cannot perceive it.

KM: Well, that's easily solved. We won't have this student write on the whole Civil War, only the South!

JB: Right. We don't allow kids to do research seriously. Whatever they write about outside of themselves winds up being farcical and by and large, lies. Teachers say that students cannot write with authority on the Battle of Appomattox, but trying to write on it teaches them to write "authoritatively" later on, which is a bunch of crap. The fact is that if you write on something you don't know you wind up in a terrible state of paralysis.

KM: It's supposed to be training.

JB: I remember as a college kid sitting up Sunday nights having to hand in a paper on Monday morning—history, philosophy, English, whatever—and I didn't know what to write because I had no knowledge of that field. No reporter writes about what he doesn't know. He sits down and writes about what he knows, and if he doesn't know it, he finds out, or his job is on the line.

KM: Some teachers say that writing about personal experience is a cop-out in composition class.

JB: I'd like to say that as an English teacher I have very high standards for writing. My students consider me nasty in the classroom. But I am not considered nasty in my relationship with students. And there's a crucial difference. I try very hard literally to love my students and to build their self-esteem.

KM: I happen to agree with you and George Dennison—who wrote *The Lives of Children*—about *love* in education. I didn't use to. Most intellectuals are scared silly of that word when it's mentioned in a school context. How do you make it possible for love to arise in a classroom?

JB: For me love is the opposite of isolation.

KM: But how can you bring about love in a classroom without being phony?

JB: There are kids in your classroom who're out to get you, and they're out to make you bleed once in a while because they feel a tremendous ego distress. A girl may have had a fight with her mother or her boyfriend. The teacher's obligation is then not to stroke back in a negative way but to allow the humanness in that person to come forward. A kid raises hell in my class. I say, "Joey, I'm feeling very angry." Then he knows how I feel, and at that point, I try to avoid negative jokes or comments. I try to avoid throwing him out of class. But if his behavior becomes absolutely intolerable, then I have to isolate the kid. I literally have to isolate him in order to make contact with him. Most of my discipline problems over the years have been kids I've been terrified of. I knew that if I made contact with them they would make me bleed. Therefore they got me. They went after me.

KM: In college, where there aren't normally these discipline problems, I still have the same feeling. Certain people are going to be out to embarrass me—particularly students who are playing the role of an "Engfishy" scholar. They're going to say in class or outside that I'm soft, that I'm not a proper authoritative scholarly sort of person. And it's always difficult for me to take that charge, whether it's true or not. I don't want the charge.

JB: "I don't want the charge." Right. You know you're going to get bitten but you don't want to get bitten. But you're a mature teacher, you have the emotional power to sustain that bite. If you don't, you're in trouble as a teacher.

KM: Is there some way you can bring about love in the classroom?

JB: Are there methods with which you can create a loving relationship between you and your kids? In the junior high and senior high? No. I'm afraid if a teacher says, "Hello John, Hello Susie, Hello Al," it's not going to help. You've gotta enjoy the kids. I don't have an answer to that.

KM: I know—and other teachers have agreed with me—that the writing of your students often carries a greater emotional intensity than writing we see by students of other high school and college teachers around the country. Do you have a method for bringing that about? How does that happen?

JB: Well, I guess I'd have to say that how intense my relationship is with a student determines the intensity of his writing. I believe I've left that stage in my life where I feel there's any answer in methodology. I have come to believe that it's my relationship with the student that determines the product. Not the mere mouthing of skills. If this is true for me, who tries desperately to communicate, can you imagine how much is communicated in a dictatorial, authoritarian, coal-mining type of classroom where they teach history? Nothing. Absolutely nothing.

KM: Let's get back to the subject of writing.

JB: When I get to the point where I must deal with the art of writing, I can now say, "Look, these standards cannot be compromised," and they understand that what I'm talking about is the standards and not their personality.

KM: You must have some students who still feel you're attacking them.

JB: Sure. The way I handle that when the writings go public and we distribute them to all the people in the class is to say that the only paper in the room that the student may not speak to is his own. Under no conditions do I ever allow a student to defend, justify, or make pronouncements on his own paper. The famous line is, "Well, what I meant to say was—." We're not interested in what you meant to say. You either got it said or you didn't. If thirty students can't figure out what you said, believe me, the problem is not with them but with you.

KM: I can imagine some teachers thinking this policy is ruthless.

JB: I've got to underline this, that holding up high standards is not difficult for a teacher *if* he is warm and loving to the children in other situations. That's why teachers should go to dances, to football games; they should go to school plays, to develop relationships with the kids outside the classroom. If the teachers are conservative robots or terrified automatons, then the kids' whole perspective on becoming adult is such that they don't want to become an adult, and rightly so.

KM: So we get violence and vandalism?

JB: Right. Human beings will get recognition. They will get it in a positive form or they will get it in a negative form, and some of the kids spend a great deal of time being very good at being very bad.

KM: How do you deal with emotionally damaged students when they come to you?

JB: The teacher's position should be to *not* reinforce bad behavior, to let the bad stroke go by without reinforcing that behavior. We had a teacher who was the meanest man on the faculty. And students said, "I really liked that teacher because he taught me to respect history. I had to sit with my hands crossed and I couldn't say a word; I was in tears most of the time, and was under tremendous pressure, but he taught me respect for history." But to me what was taught, if anything, was not respect but fear. What the kid learned was that those things which he had a negative perception on, how his world was created, were reinforced by this man.

KM: Getting back to writing, if you don't believe in objective measurement of writing, how do you judge your effect on students?

JB: Well, if when they come in, they're unaware, and when they leave they're more aware, then something has happened through their writing, through their analysis of writing in the classroom, or through their observations of reality.

KM: You're talking about students objectifying their experience.

JB: Yes. Any act that is objectified from our psyche, our subconscious, or even our conscious world is a personal creation, a work of art. It may be a bad work of art, a lousy work of art, but it's still a work of art. It's no longer ours.

KM: And because it's no longer ours, we can talk about it. Are there other ways of measuring your success as a teacher?

JB: If I'm able to maintain a relationship with a child for 180 days and keep it. A warm, friendly relationship beginning on the first day, and on the last day when they leave, a continued warm, friendly relationship. Now if you can do that it's an accomplishment because you know relationships between people go up and down and in and out.

KM: And you wouldn't have been able to maintain that relationship if you hadn't been open-minded and learned something from that child.

JB: Right—having sustained a relationship for a length of time with an adult, and preferably on an adult level. One of the nice things is that we can sit down with a piece of writing from anybody—Hemingway, Steinbeck—and talk about it in class, and the remarks are revelations to me as a teacher.

KM: I've had that experience in a Shakespeare class.

JB: It's a combined thing. They look at Shakespeare without your knowledge. You give your knowledge, and you put their perspective in with your knowledge and at the end of the class some of the observations that come out are really brand-new.

KM: The experiences of the teacher and the students speak to each other.

JB: And my experience has to be defended and put up to scrutiny and rejected by the young adults so that when they take that outside the classroom it is clarified in their mind exactly what that position is, so—ironically—it can be accepted into their psyche.

KM: Then they're really listening to what you say.

JB: Yeah. But the most stunning comment about my teaching is that I don't listen any more.

KM: Who says that?

JB: Oh, the kids. "You're not listening to me, Mr. Bennett. Will you shut up for a minute and let me say something?" But, by the way, it's the freedom to say that in class that indicates that you're OK. In addition, it means that we care enough to value your opinion, so shut up and listen to us.

KM: That is one of the things that happens when the teacher becomes older. I have a friend who's finding that his students' good observations are becoming boring to him, not because they're not perceptive, but because he's heard them so many times from other students.

JB: Yeah, so I really have to maintain a naiveté.

KM: I want to get back to what you say to students about their work. I think we lost that somewhere.

JB: I say, "I want a focused writing on your childhood, or a parent, or an incident at school, a conflict writing, a tension writing. Give me a situation where you were involved with somebody else and I feel your tension. Write on that five times, five days, about ten or fifteen minutes. And then choose one of those writings to go public." Then we get into the actual skills. You know if about the fourth time the guy is still spelling every third word wrong—although I put little emphasis on this—I might say, "Now look, will you (the writer's not named, remember) do me a favor and look words up for the next assignment, since the other people here and I can't understand what you're saying because you're not spelling the words right." The point of correct spelling is to make writing readable, not to set up a series of spelling words to be learned by rote and forgotten. The fact is that spelling is an organic part of writing. We *do* get to mechanics, we *do* worry about grammar, we *do* worry about sentence structure, but we do it as it comes up for each child. For instance, if a kid doesn't spell the words wrong and if he doesn't have any sentence structure problems, I don't say anything about those matters. Why make everybody suffer?

KM: The assignments are open, but they are located in the child's reality?

JB: That's what I'm saying. OK, the kid comes in and writes a personal assignment. He can say anything he wants, he can spell any way he wants, he can use any sort of bad language he wants. He gives it to me and I scan it. I've got two things I put on those writings. One is I might put parentheses around content. The subject might be good, but the writing stinks and I want him to know that the content might be OK to use in the future. The other thing—I might underline something. That indicates that the sentence zings, is powerful.

KM: It sounds sensible, and therefore easy in a way.

JB: I must say this: the first four, five, or six weeks of class are painful for students who have never had to write the truth or never had the opportunity. They begin to take the first steps in writing the truth and we say, "But you're not writing the truth." That brings into perspective the fact that what a person thinks is the truth is not necessarily the truth for an audience, and not even necessarily the truth for the writer on second thought.

KM: This suggests that the conventional teacher, who seldom sees truth that counts for the writer, must live a miserable life.

JB: The most paralyzing thing is for a teacher to face 120 papers written on a subject, and everybody is writing on something of which they have little knowledge. After you read the first five papers, they are all the same, and yet you must dig through 115 more papers saying the same thing. Can you think of anything more ghastly? After a while the teacher becomes mechanized, because it never dawns on him that perhaps he's asking the kid to write about something of which he has no knowledge. And if he has no knowledge, then he will lie; and some kids are smart at lying and therefore get good grades, and some kids are not smart at lying and they will get bad grades. Writing is not a matter of intelligence; it's a matter of using the vocabulary you have in a germane, powerful, clear, precise way. If you've a very small vocabulary, you can still use it with amazing power. And if you have a very large vocabulary, you can do likewise.

KM: Mr. Bennett, you don't seem to realize that we are preparing students for professional lives when they will be constantly reporting on things they don't know well. And that may be the test—that we will send them off to Cleveland in order to make a report on something they don't know about and we don't know about, so that we will then know about it. So what are you going to say to that line?

JB: It's true that we will have to deal with problems we have very few answers to, if any. That's a fact. But it's important that we teach the child to approach the problem with that understanding instead of thinking, "I will BS my way through this thing and everything will come out all right." It won't come out all right. It's much easier to write, "I don't know," than it is to write, "There are certain characteristics and aspects of the plot of *Huckleberry Finn.* . . ." The teacher should make the child aware of what are lies and what is the truth, his personal truth. But if the teacher lies, then it becomes difficult for the child to maintain his optimism about growing up. "My God, if they're all liars, and this is what I have to grow up to, why grow up? Well, I'll build a cocoon."

KM: You make me realize how tremendously I may be influencing a young person when I do the smallest thing in the classroom.

JB: If the teacher is insensitive, if the teacher cannot solve problems, if the teacher cannot perceive the child's reality or perceive his own reality, the system breaks down and what we have is isolated ice cubes in the icebox, each one locked in his own little ice tray, and nobody communicates with anybody, and so the child walks out feeling that education is a waste of time, which of course it is, under this system.

KM: I shudder at that responsibility.

JB: I say the English teacher is the most powerful teacher in the world because he's the only one who can deal with the human heart in conflict with itself. If that teacher is a liar, a hypocrite, then the whole basis of our culture falls apart.

Assignment 6

HENRY B. MALONEY

Communication 103
Fall, 1984
Dr. Murray Singledorf,
Instructor

Assignment 6.

During the first month of your freshman term here at South Stateland University, the Communication course has aimed at sharp-
ening your powers of observation and expression so that you can
express your ideas with more detail and clarity. At this point
you should be prepared to give your impression of some aspect of
campus life. You may fulfill this assignment in one of the following ways:

(a) Prepare either a scripted or an unscripted dialogue or conversation with one or more of your fellow students.

(b) Write an essay giving your observations.

(c) Write an appropriate poem or folk song.

(d) Prepare a pantomime.

(e) Write a one-act play.

(f) Use another form of communication not specified above.

This assignment is due October 7.

Communication 103
Assignment 6
October 7, 1984

Dear Professor Singledorf,

After carefully mulling over your list of options, I have decided
on "(f) use another form of communication not specified above." As you
have probably noticed by now, the form in which I'll describe my impres-
sions of South Stateland U. is a personal letter. I did give serious
thought to choosing (b), the essay, but frankly, your deck seems to be
stacked against it. In the list of lively, modern-looking options you've provided, the essay stands by itself as a path for old thinkers to gallumph
along in their granny dresses. So, to save my Bacon, gradewise, I have decided on a rasher approach than (b) affords. That choice should be worth
a few brownie points going in, and my cozying up to you in a friendly
letter should be worth a few more.

At the risk of becoming *too* intimate, let me add to our growing rapport by telling you that I expect to become an English teacher some day. Not college; high school. And even though a friendly letter allows for a certain amount of rambling, I won't give you my reasons for that decision now since there is a Topic to be dealt with. (If one of your subsequent assignments "fits" what I'd like to tell you, I'll write the reasons later in the term. I think they're pretty good, especially when compared with the quasi-humanitarian values of my brother, who wants to become a rich M.D.)

Now, the observations. What better way to score another half brownie point than by writing about Communication 103? (Frankly, Prof. S., I was never this turned on about scoring points before getting into a class with two Jocks [who will be discussed later] and listening to the nonhumanitarian side of my quasi-humanitarian brother [whom you met in the paragraph above]. I'm afraid those exposures have dulled a few of my nobler impulses.) Some of my observations are rather critical of my classmates or more precisely, of the educational system that produced my classmates. However, these negative comments are included in this friendly letter because I trust your judgment in recognizing that this is a letter to you, Professor Singledorf, not an open letter to the class. Unhappily, I must stress this point because I've been burned a few times in the past by teachers. There was, for example, the seventh grade teacher who ate her lunch in the classroom so she could pry into our "confidential" journals, which we had been assured no one would see. Frankly, if I had intended writing for a broader audience, I would have changed the salutation to something like "Dear Prof. Singledorf et al.," and made my observations much blander. But since Assignment 6 did not state that our remarks must be shared with classmates, I'd like to postpone that opportunity. (If you are still scoring the brownie game, score two for increased intimacy through designated privacy, but subtract a point for my seemingly antisocial stance.)

My observations are divided into two broad categories, *People* and *Stuff*. Under *People*, I have included my twenty-four classmates. I have not included Me because the whole landscape of a friendly letter is contoured by the writer. More Me than that you need not. (You see; there is the wordplay Me blossomming on that landscape.) *Stuff*, at this point in the course, includes the textbook and the assignments.

If you had not provided time for class members to introduce themselves at the first meeting, many of my observations of my fellow students probably would have been superficial and speculative. But since I have some idea of who they are, I think that I am able to read them a bit. To begin with, there are the two Jocks, Harris and Minton. I gather from reading the sport pages of the *South Stateland Statement* that Harris is just good enough to have received an athletic scholarship but not good enough to think of pro football as a career. Audrey Minton, five feet eleven in her socks, is a first-rate basketball player who can probably look forward to making a few bucks playing in a women's semipro league when she graduates. In fact, she may have been born at the right time. Women's basketball could become profitable soon since the enforcers of Title IX have finally given the TV networks a deadline by which they must substantially increase their coverage of women's sports. I would say that Harris and Minton probably perform in this class in a narrow range that extends from C– to C+ since they seem adequate in writing and talking. From what I observe, they read and understand the essays in the textbook. But, alas, my good Singledorf, their bloody spirits lie in thrall to a couple of leather bags bloated with air. No one has planted any poetry seeds in their souls. And, as a consequence, on those two occasions when Communication 103 came face to face with poems by William Stafford and May Swenson, there was no stirring, no hum from Harris or Minton. There was instead that kind of embarrassed, xenophobic backing off that one might experience if a Martian emerged from the next stall in the john. Now, I ask you, Professor, how can Harris and Minton realize a high percentage of their human potential if no one has planted and nurtured a few poetry seeds in their souls? Between you and me, I've started storing those seeds already, and by the time I get into high school teaching I'll have so many varieties that none of my students' souls will be able to resist the posies proffered by Theresa Poetryseed—but that is material for a later assignment.

I reckon that we have about five Bus Ad majors in here. That's counting Hurley, who says he's going to major in Math but already is earning a fortune as a supplier of precooked popcorn for sporting events and movie theaters. (There is a rumor that Hurley has five warehouses filled with popcorn in preparation for the next remake of *Star Wars,* which doesn't open until Thanksgiving.) Unlike the Jocks, who may not be able to look beyond the excitement of here and now, the Bizads are peering far down the road. They've studied what they will need to become successful, and, come hell or high water, they're going to make it. (If you are still wearing your English teacher's hat, Prof, you may have moved reflexively to circle "hell or high water" and write "cliché" beside it. I hope you have buried that hat for the duration of this friendly letter. But, if not, how about perceiving "hell or high water" as a metaphor for poetry. After all, at this point in time, it's rather dead [Oops! You aren't one of those people who see "dead" as an absolute, are you?] as a cliché, but does offer the poetic attributes of alliteration and contrast.) My point is that the Bizads have no place in their life scenarios for poetry. For them, poetry is a siren attempting to seduce them away from their goal of becoming successful in business.

Could Theresa Poetryseed have touched their souls in high school? Well, why not? You see, poetry to me is more than what meters the eye. It's a different plate of beans from becoming an expert on Frost, or analyzing the moderns, or studying the roots of the Harlem Renaissance. I know that's what you college people do, and that's cool if you want to do it. But poetry to me is not scholarship about poetry. It's an individualizing spirit that grows in souls and nudges the body to use expressive words that genuinely reflect the uniqueness of a certain human being. Poetry is a song of yourself that can be sung, played, danced, pantomimed, or acted out in your day-to-day behavior. It may even be performed in a friendly letter. In my poetic world, it's not relevant whether that song is set forth in a fashion that you fellows label prose, or whether it's served with a heavier sprinkling of white space and called poetry—or even whether it's put into words.

Meanwhile, back to Communication 103. The Jocks are consequences of the educational system because unless South Stateland U. recruits Jocks skilled enough to attract 350,000 ticket buyers to the football stadium, the athletic program falls short of its goal, and, fiscally speaking, the penalty for falling short is too painful to contemplate. Bizads are molded by a larger societal system than education. Their form of dying is cast by the financial rewards and status provided by our society in general. Both Jocks and Bizads have serious problems, but in my humble judgment, the students most badly shafted by the educational system are the MinComPoops—Philby, Hartung, Adams, and Klostenberg. Adams appears older because he's taller, but I'd bet one of my precious poetry books that none of the four has seen his fifteenth birthday yet. I presume that they took the Minimum Competency Test for high school graduation, earned a passing score, and were given a diploma and booted out of school by the state, which has maintained that passing the test demonstrates that one has assimilated a high school education. Cognitively speaking, that may be true. But on a maturity line, I would calculate the distance between 14 years of age and 18 as being equal to the distance between orange jello and a parfait. The MinComPoops are nice enough kids, I guess, and they appear to be book smart, but how in the world can you sow any real poetry in those immature, inexperienced little souls? I suppose they'll get jobs when they grow up, but my guess is that there will be a void in the amount of human potential they can realize because they missed an important stage in their development. No teacher has ever opened them up to metaphor, and by the time they discover the lack, they will be so set on achieving their life goals they will consider the pursuit of poetry a foolish diversion.

So far I have categorized about half the class and indicated that I think they've missed the bus of the Muse. Now, I'll peer into the crystal ball and suggest what lies ahead for them. A fair number of them—and others like them—will become school board members, after campaigning on a "no frills, let's really teach basics" ticket. They will then use whatever clout they can manage to see that their school systems hire grammar experts to teach English classes instead of flakes like Theresa Poetryseed.

"Oh, what she does is interesting, but I see no value, no *real* purpose in it."

"I wonder if she ever considered becoming a kindergarten teacher."

"Her high school principal said she was a little hard to control. I hardly think that's the kind of person we wish to place in front of impressionable young students."

"She's probably overcompensating for having an old-fashioned name like Theresa."

There is some hope for the third group I see in this class, the six preprofessionals. Maybe the Prepros can absorb more material because they have more smarts than the rest if us. (Check those SAT scores, Prof. I'll bet you'll find them a few notches higher.) Whether they're headed for Law or Medicine or whatever, they seem to want to fulfill their human potential as far as they can. Poetry? Sure. Faulkner? OK. They appear to read both with insight. Now I don't know which came first, their multifaceted interests in life or their aspirations to work in the professions. And even though I respect most of their viewpoints more than I do my brother's, I don't know that I would prefer to have one of them snip out my appendix. What I want in that (hypothetical, I hope) situation is the most skilled technician. But for the Country, Civilization, the Culture—in short, when it comes to the Big Picture—I want to be mingling with a group of human beings who are interested in generating and responding to poetic impulses.

The other seven students in Communication 103 would fall into some general, catch-all category like Miscellaneous. A kind word for them would be Explorers. A less kind but more apt word is Wanderers. They're here because in their minds they can picture themselves nowhere but in college. They impinge on my future goal because I see them as tomorrow's parents, frightened by innovation (even though tomorrow *is* innovation) and seeking to maintain the joys of a *status quo* that doesn't look to me to be all that joyous, unless one is so emotionally sterile that he equates painlessness with joy.

(Maybe one day I'll write a one-act, one-character play about someone who runs for the school board because she's poetry-minded and believes the impulses of poetry should be heard and experienced in the schools. I'll call it "Meter Maid" and possibly dedicate it to you, good Prof., tra la.)

From conversations with my friends I find that it's fashionable to say that the textbooks for the freshman communication courses are absolute dogs. Our book isn't great, but it's not that bad. Its purpose, I trust, is to infuse us with common experiences for writing and discussion so that we're all starting from the same base. You know, of course, Professor S., that it's a pseudocommon base. Since half of the essays I've read have been extremely uninteresting, I have had to manufacture responses to them. Either I say something that I think you will appreciate or I take a seemingly far-out position and try to dazzle you with the logic of my defense strategy, figuring that the technique alone is worth a few points. (This isn't meant to be a confessional paper, or an exposé in which the magician reveals to the onlooker just how the woman in the cabinet avoids being skewered by long knives. It is rather a lament that we have to engage in these writing games and that I am compelled by the system to hitch a line onto various vehicles to show you that I can write.)

I can appreciate your problem in having to plant common experiences among people who are quite unalike (see preceding paragraphs). My goal is to help you by releasing some of their human potential so that they will at least hum together to poetic impulses by the time they get to this level of education. And, with the exception of the MinComPoops, I believe I can. The MinComPoops are destined to disappear as soon as lawmakers see that they can eliminate a faulty statute and still save face. Then these kids can mature in an appropriate setting.

Your assignments, Prof., show that you believe that some of us are individuals, but I don't think you know quite what to do with that knowledge. We've written an autobiographical paper, responses to three essays, and an exploration of today's morality. The last one might have soared to the sky if you had encouraged us to look at morality in the context of a career we could envision for ourselves. For example, *Winning at What Cost?* for the Jockos; *Exploiting the Consumer to Realize a Profit,* for the Bizads; and so on. Frankly, I didn't offer you much on that assignment because I didn't know at that time whether you would give my paper a sincere reading. But I could have expatiated on the inconsequential, dull, unpoetic experiences being foisted off on kids in the name of high school English. (For alternative approaches, haul out your dictionary of antonyms. For ways of implementing these alternatives, examine the literature for ways of effecting change in the system before the anti-crap-elimination sensors cause the red lights to start blinking and the sirens to scream.)

The variety of ways in which we may respond to Assignment 6 suggests that each of us will choose a comfortable mode of expression. There's a touch of my kind of poetry in that assignment, Sir, even though some will view it as a license to be frivolous. In a way, it is indeed an opportunity to be frivolous—for one-fifteenth of the course requirements.

Well, Murray, old shoe, that's about it. After reading this far you know that I haven't approached you familiarly because I need some kind of counseling on a personal problem. Nor should you interpret my friendly language as an attempt to tease you into a meeting in your office with the hope that you'll put your hand on my leg and an A on my report card. I just wanted to say something as a person since your approach to this class has begun to indicate that you are genuinely concerned about people communicating with each other as individuals. Also, it is apparent that you respond to poetry.

When you come right down to basics, the kind of English teacher I want to be is someone a student might write a friendly letter to, as well as a person he would try to write a well-crafted, objective paper for. I think a friendly letter is friendly only insofar as it is a personal voice —an individual bray or strut or wail or goose, whatever. It's a human reaction to the inroads of the technological society with its look-alike compositions, accurately written, but stamped out on an assembly line. I can manufacture these kinds of faceless papers as I demonstrated on Assignments 3 and 4. But they are not me. As an English teacher, I know I'll have an obligation to help students develop a certain proficiency in putting out this kind of product, but all the while I want poetry seeds to start growing in their souls so they can get the satisfaction of hearing their own voices.

My last word, Myrrh, is this. I deliberately set out to write a paper that you could not appropriately give a letter grade to or even "correct," in the traditional English teacher sense. A teacher would have to be an incorrigible pedant to stick a grade on a friendly letter. A comment, an observation, a response, a wry remark (hold the ham; there's been enough already) perhaps, but no grade, or we've stopped being people and succumbed to the system. If that ever happens, I'd be compelled to revert to spilling you the same slop as the MinComPoops, the Jocks, the Bizads, and the Miscellaneous people, and what a dispiriting experience that would be.

Very sincerely,
Theresa

P. S. You can put your English teacher's hat back on now. I've misspelled one word, just to be insouciant. (Score two points for creating an occasion to use a fine old word one rarely sees today.)

T.

P. P. S. After some careful reflection, good reader Singledorf, I decided not to include any comments about you in the *People* section. The format I have chosen implies that I perceive you to be trustworthy and responsible. I believe you are. I believe that you are also discerning, so that three years hence when you receive a recommendation form that asks you to describe my strengths and weaknesses as a potential high school English teacher, you will be able to underscore a noble trait or two while concealing my varied shortcomings in a couple of obscure sentences fashioned in unreadably dull rhetoric.

(Not Gil) T.

Literature: The Basis for Curricular Design

MILDRED WEBSTER

As I consider the almost immediate future, it seems to me that teaching English in that future does not have to be vastly different from the best teaching of the 1930s or 40s or 50s or 60s or 70s. Of course, there are styles of teaching that follow fads or go with the times, but the three most important elements likely to be required in the future—as in the past—will be students, teachers, and teaching materials.

The students of ten or twenty or thirty years from now will probably be less book-minded than those of twenty years ago; likely they will have a background culled from television watching and from the media-oriented classrooms of the past years. Just as libraries have cut down on book budgets and added other departments, so the young people have expanded their ways of learning. Teachers of the future, too, will have developed ways of using the wide range of exciting materials at hand (if they are not driven into the box of all the substitutes for composition: traditional grammar drill, mindless workbooks, and writing drawn exclusively from personal experience). Teachers can expect to have more resources in the libraries and the classrooms. The explosion of materials and expansion of choices of the past several decades have so enriched learning and the teaching environment that what has always been basic to English teaching should be universally attainable.

What is basic? In my view it is literacy: The imaginative insight of the reader is joined with oral and written expression so that the student is able to share personal insights with others.

The study of literature is more appealing to adolescents (and to graduate students) if the reader has some confidence in his ability to reach respectable conclusions about the worth of a piece of literature to himself and to a literate society. Whenever one comes to grips with a piece of literature, there are three valid approaches: One, the student can ask and seek to discover what the author had in mind when he created his artistic work; two, the student can seek to discover the collected opin-

47

ions of many scholars and critics who have studied and thought about the work (which, in the case of Shakespeare or T. S. Eliot or a host of others, can be considerable and may represent a broad range of ideas or a comforting consensus); and, three, one can recognize personal insights that come to the first-time reader—even when he is a student in one's classroom.

The best literature, at any point in education, is like an onion. When the outer layers have been removed, there are many more—layer upon layer. The layers differ for elementary, middle school, junior high, senior high, undergraduate, and graduate students. No one has ever considered that Lamb's *Tales from Shakespeare* takes all of the magic out of seeking the essence of *King Lear;* the many translations of the *Iliad* and the *Odyssey* can increase in meaning and impact the final translation by the student of Greek. At each school level there should be an appropriate kind of study suited to the sophistication and ability of the student. Each teacher should find the layer of response appropriate to his class.

During the years following sputnik, there was an explosion in high school English teaching—an explosion in methods, purposes, and materials —that pretty well blew out of the English curriculum much that had been traditional, and in places it has left the English program fragmented. I maintain that the fragmentation is not disastrous if the *teacher* has not become fragmented but continues to view English as a whole in which the unrelated bits can find a place. Basically, the result has been an enrichment and a freedom in choice and method. It is still too early to judge all the outcomes, and it may just be possible that all of the pieces let loose by the elective explosion will come back to the educational earth in the shape of a beautiful composite.

From my past teaching, I want to put together a unit of study that can furnish the framework for applying my thinking to a classroom situation. This is a unit that combines the old—Chaucer and a brief look at the emerging modern English just before it took the real turn to its present shape—and the new, in some of the literature representative of modern philosophy. For Chaucer, the teacher is likely to be on firm ground; Chaucer has been around long enough for a wide range of study materials to have found a place in high school libraries and classrooms. For the modern literature of alienation, satire, and existentialism, the teacher and class can break intellectual ground together.

The class that I shall envision will be like those I have taught: eighteen-year-olds in the twelfth grade, able students for the most part, willing to be interested or turned off, and ready to express personal thoughts and opinions.

For the seniors, I prefer starting with the present and moving back to the past; in the years when the anthology organized the course of study, I liked to reorganize and start at the back of the book. For this juxtaposition of Middle English and Chaucerian past with the existential present, I believe that more valid comparisons can be made by going back to 1400 for the starting point. Why have I chosen these? In total recognition of vast oversimplifications, I shall look at the Chaucerian end of the Middle Ages as a time when English and European society was dominated by class rigidity and religious preoccupation. It was also a period of emerging change in politics, religion, language, and just about everything else. We are also living in a time of rapid change and fluid values, and goodness knows the language world is changing as we become a less print-dominated society.

Given a world of change—1400 or 2000—how easy it is for us to identify with Chaucer's characters on their way to Canterbury and with many of the characters of modern literature even when they are caught in their private interior monologues. Chaucer's pilgrims accept their society even while recognizing its faults; they accept the church even while admitting to its hypocrisies; and they accept their own places in their imperfect universe. We of the twentieth century can also identify, in part, with Vladimir and Estragon as they attempt to make sense out of a personal world that waits for Godot, without being quite sure what the present means or the future holds.

In preparation for any study, I need dozens of books. For reference and for browsing there should be from five to ten books for each student. I first will look around the classroom, then I will look to my own store of books, and finally I will raid the library for books on the 1066 to 1485 period—literature and history, history of the language, and books by and about Chaucer. Books at several reading levels will be accumulated and made available for the study. Students can be encouraged to look at home for college texts that a parent or sibling may have studied. Paperbacks, such as R. M. Lumiansky's *Chaucer's Canterbury Tales* (Washington Square Press, 1960), will be a favorite personal acquisition for some students. In my collection of schoolroom books are a variety of textbooks left over from the days when the anthology set the boundaries in high school and undergraduate English study. Many of these are excellent reference books that can be rescued from discard and purchased at used-book prices.

To move back in time, students need to immerse themselves in the atmosphere of the past. Initial discussion would include putting together some of the entertainment experiences of the past ten years or so.

- Who has seen the movies *Becket* and *A Lion in Winter?*

- Who has seen Robin Hood in some of the television presentations?

- Who has record collections that include border ballads?

- Who has read books with historical backgrounds?

- Has anyone seen and heard the dramatic presentation of *Chaucer's Tales?* (Some college drama departments have presented it, and some students—to my surprise—may have seen this in London or New York.)

To give focus to the background reading I will offer the students a list of dates, historical events, people of the period, and literary characters and literary forms: *1066, the Norman Invasion, serfs, squires, Wars of the Roses, priory, John Wyclif, Eleanor of Aquitaine, Chaucer, mystery and miracle plays, metrical romances,* and so on. Such a list helps to focus reading, to reinforce remembering, and to develop the knowledge of the backgrounds necessary to appreciate and understand *The Canterbury Tales.*

It may take a week to do the digging and note-taking to acquire the background. Certainly there will be time for the teacher to help each student with individual searching and interpreting. When I have students work at something like this, I am pleased and amazed at how good the expository writing can be; compression, directness, and clarity are the usual qualities; "correctness"' is not an empty adherence to grammatical tradition. Good discussion can be interrupted by listening to a recording of *Camelot* and then placing this modern musical into the framework of the Arthurian metrical romance.

Next comes the literature. I like to provide every student with his personal Middle English copy of Chaucer to be used as a potential "pony," once it is overwritten with current words, marked up in class, and used as part of open-notebook testing. This copy can also be used in conjunction with a variety of modern translations, many of which can be located in the book collection in the classroom. For the first day or two, I will spend class time reading from the Middle English and ad libbing a translation. Class discussion will center on the initial *fact* study; students can contribute information about Thomas à Becket for starters. The training of the medieval knight and the geographical implications of the Crusades can be drawn upon for amplifying Chaucer's description of the knight, the foremost pilgrim.

For those who have taken a liking to Chaucer's people and tales, this is a good time to make a study of a tale and a character and think and write a bit about how the two interrelate. Other students may prefer to go in search of medieval music and art. Some may be drawn to architecture and art, others to the homely arts of costume and housekeeping. This is a time to allow for reaching out. Students who are just tolerating the Middle Ages should be allowed to read something that appeals to them. Each of these brief individual projects should result in a written or oral report to the class.

Some of the textbooks and anthologies of the 1930s and 1940s were directed toward more sophisticated literary interests and to the student with no reading problems and the usual composition problems. In these books I have found a more thoughtful kind of questioning. These I adapt and use for discussion, which allows each year's students to make use of current interests and opinions. For instance, from 1969 to 1971, one could question why the people of Europe went off to the Crusades or the Hundred Years' War with such a willingness for immolation—as contrasted with the more enlightened self-interest of those who rejected the war in Vietnam; in the 1980s, the high school student may feel no identification with the emotions and reactions of those persons fifteen years older. In fact, the eighteen-year-old most likely would not bother to inquire into the previous thinking of the older generation, now in its thirties.

The conclusion of this study will focus on the history of the language. We will go back to Anglo-Saxon and find out what a good high school text has to report, and we will explore some of the books that have been aimed at high school students rather than at the translators of *Beowulf*. Along with the books, recordings will be of great help in reproducing the sounds of a reconstructed past. Students who are deeply involved with modern or ancient language study may be attracted to the grammar of Old and Middle English, but this is not as interesting to most students as vocabulary. Language study can be pursued as far as resources will permit and as far as student interest will take it; for most students it will hold passing interest, with a strong "take it or leave it" reaction, but once in a while there is the one student who gets hooked.

The second portion of this teaching unit deals with modern materials and will include some poetry, a few short stories, and two plays. For short stories I will include James Joyce's "Araby," Albert Camus's "The Guest," and Katherine Mansfield's "The Garden Party." Others could be added or substituted, but these present three arresting characters: the young boy of "Araby" reaching out in fantasy to the adolescent and adult prisoned inside him; Camus's teacher, forced to come to grips with a gamut of thoughts and emotions which he is only half ready to confront; and the privileged young woman, half girl, half child, of "The

Garden Party," who is uneasily moving from the protection of class and limited life experience to "hold hands" with death and to move across the safety of social tracks. All these present identifiable emotions, experiences, and reactions to high school seniors. They also provide a limited comparison with the *Prologue*'s squire.

So much of modern poetry speaks to the problems and themes of twentieth century philosophy that choosing and limiting become a problem. But there are some poets and poems that have had great impact as I have taught them or allowed the poets to teach or to speak. In the 1960s, English teachers were given tremendous help in the presentation of poetry by the application of literary criticism, by adapting the inductive way of teaching, and by employing close reading. The explication of contemporary poems, a feature of *The English Journal,* gave many teachers a useful model to follow for study beyond the textbooks. Some of the poems that I find thought-provoking and interesting to study include D. H. Lawrence's "Snake"; Theodore Roethke's' "The Waking"; Randall Jarrell's "The Death of the Ball Turret Gunner"; T. S. Elliot's "Sweeney Among the Nightingales"; William Butler Yeats's "Sailing to Byzantium" and "The Second Coming."

It is no accident that Yeats's "The Second Coming" is last. "Surely some revelation is at hand" can lead to open speculation on what this revelation might be. "Things fall apart; the centre cannot hold" is so easy to illustrate with events of the century. Then one can go to art, music, philosophy, and literature of the twentieth century, and for a time a class can try to verbalize what the center should be. Is it harmony between man and his fellow man and nature? Is it security? What is security? Contrast modern man, at the center of an explosion that makes him think that his world is coming apart, with men of Chaucer's time, who— at least in the literature—seem much more at home in a period that is soon to be replaced by a whole new set of values and directions. What is there for a high school senior to identify with today? Is identification to be at a physical and emotional level or can people reach out for intellectual and philosophical identification? What will happen today and tomorrow to help us do something about our dilemmas? What will stimulate tomorrow's society to evaluate and improve the human condition?

It is against such paradoxes of the times that we will look at, read, and think about two dramas and a painting. The picture is Edvard Munch's *The Scream* (1893), on display in the National Gallery in Oslo, Norway, and reproduced in many modern art books. The two plays we shall study are Eugene Ionesco's *The Rhinoceros* and Samuel Beckett's *Waiting for Godot.*

The Rhinoceros was first written as a short story, and if it is available, I would prefer to start with the story version. My class and

I will talk about surrealism, the philosophical "absurd," and symbolic realism. The play can be read in class with a discussion of staging and interpretation of parts. There exist a great many ideas and levels for discussion—some obvious, some abstruse and sophisticated. Is society as disoriented as Ionesco suggests? For whom is Berenger speaking when he says, "I feel out of place in life, among people . . ."? Can an eighteen-year-old accept the premise that "a return to primal integrity" will solve the problems of a world succumbing to the herd instinct? (What will this do to television advertising?—or any advertising?—or even English teaching?) While *Rhinoceros* seems to be asking big, open questions about conformity and individualism, the play will leave us with the big, open question of what it is to be human and what is the human condition—now, and twenty years from now.

We will set the play *Rhinoceros* against Chaucer's time and ask some questions, for discussion and for individual written comment. How does conformity work in any period? What is the effect of philosophical beliefs and movements, such as the medieval church or modern existentialism? Someone in class is certain to suggest that the framework may not be right: How are we, today, to know that Chaucer's pilgrims are so one-dimensional and that the proto-characters of modern drama are so multidimensional? As a teacher I am usually gratified at student response and fascinated by class discussions.

As an interim step, before confronting *Godot,* I will direct my class to take a closer look at Edvard Munch's *Scream.* This painting—of surrealistic red and yellow sky reflected in blue water, of a road with two shadowy and indistinct figures in the background, and of the cry from the figure in the foreground—combines artistic disorder with symbolic sound. Munch said of his picture that it suggested "inner agitation." As they contemplate their future—the world of 2000—a class of seniors might find ample reasons for the terror of the cry and for Munch's "inner agitation."

My class and I have come a long way from the group of thirty or so pilgrims starting out for Canterbury Cathedral on a fine English April morning six hundred years ago. We shall conclude this unit by locating ourselves on another road, where, with Estragon and Vladimir, we shall be *Waiting for Godot.*

Waiting for Godot has a good many advantages for students. First, the play has not developed a critical consensus, and second, the reader or theatergoer is not certain of what the author has intended him to think. A third advantage is the ignorance of the teacher on these same matters. It was not until I discovered that teachers in England were including *Waiting for Godot* in their upper grade curriculum that I decided to be daring and try it too. Totally unencumbered by scholarly and critical conclusions, I could almost agree with the line from the play and from student reactions, "Nothing happens, nobody comes, nobody goes, it's awful." Compare this with Chaucer's pilgrims who knew what they were going to do, who would be traveling with them, where they would go, and even—after their evening at the Tabard Inn—what they would be doing for entertainment on the way.

We set the certainty of Chaucer's *Prologue* against the background of *Godot,* and what do we have? The play is fixed in time, but the two evenings seem unreal; the setting is a road, but that road appears to be unreal and symbolic. Then there are the characters; they, too, seem to be more symbolic than real. While the dramatic experience seems grounded in reality, here is the ultimate of surrealism. If the class attempts to analyze the characters, Vladimir and Estragon appear to be obvious and uncomplicated, Lucky and Pozzo seem to be two-dimensional, and the boy messenger is like a stock character out of Greek drama. We will read the play; we will attempt to analyze it; we will recognize its obscurities; and we will try to understand the symbolism of it. Since I do not have an interpretation from college notes, I will have students, working alone or in groups, develop a variety of possible symbol systems. The play has the advantage of surface simplicity, but like any good play it possesses layers of complexity. We shall work only on the outer layer of this onion.

For a first-time teaching experience with *Waiting for Godot* I needed to develop some class activities. The search for background yielded little; magazines from the 1950s when the play had been reviewed were no longer available. A nearby university library provided a helpful casebook and a few brief items in the reference section. Some of the assignments were these:

- Summarize the play and give the action of each of the two acts.

- Characterize the four characters of the play.

- Select three quotations that you think carry the philosophy of the play. Discuss these in relation to the play.

- How do you view *Godot?* Is your view drawn from the play or is it shaped by your imagination?

- Take a standard definition of tragi-comedy and apply it to the play.

- What is the picture of time that emerges from the play? Does this have a relation to the coming on of night? Is time a symbolism? If you see time as symbolic rather than real, what is it a symbol of?

When a class of bright high school seniors brings to the class session some concrete answers to even abstract questions, the pooling of ideas is wondrous. Probably half of the class that studied *Waiting for Godot* was amply ready, and the other half was willing to be involved. I concluded the unit with an essay test, and every student had something to write on each of the statements or questions. When I asked for a symbolic pattern for the play, I received as many ideas as there were students in the class. When I gave a quotation and asked for a reaction and support for the idea, I was pleased at the quality of the thinking.

Since the play has been presented on television, I now have a taped, dramatic reading of *Godot;* there is an early recording available. Seeing the play or listening to a dramatic reading will be of help to the unimaginative; the creative reader can probably do as well without the help. At the discussion end, *Waiting for Godot* is a wonder. As one listens to the repetitiveness, the unreality of the realism, and the manipulation of language, it may just be that Beckett is leading us back to another kind of sanity through the distortion in his play.

The teacher of tomorrow will have experienced some of the great traumas of this century first hand. This has been a time of political and social change and upheaval, of atomic threat and promise. No wonder literature has become disoriented and has turned in on itself. This has been a century in which earlier promises have peaked and faded as liberty, democracy, and individualism have floundered and become disordered.

Writers, reformers, and revolutionaries of the future may seek to bring harmony into the social and political universe and to impose order on the aesthetic disarray of the arts of literature, music, art, architecture, and even dance. Possibly the artistic revolution that began a hundred years ago in painting has run its course, just as teachers in the classroom have become comfortable with its literary output. The subjective "isms" of a century may be giving way to a new objectivity, a concreteness that will be neither absurd, nor imitative, nor violently distorted in time and space. The teacher of English may find a new literature that imposes logic on distorted time and surrealistic place.

In the meanwhile, look again at Chaucer's *Prologue* and set his characters against Vladimir, Estragon, Pozzo, and Lucky as they wait for a Godot who does not come. The pilgrims will push on to a real Canterbury as far into the future as we can see.

Future Grammar

JEAN MALMSTROM

Our Puritan heritage has saddled us with a national mania for correctness. In the matters of speaking and writing, correctness is traditionally equated with grammar, which is popularly regarded as the stairway to success in our upwardly mobile society.

Even though no universally accepted definition of grammar exists, the public agrees that grammar should be taught by English teachers to make their students write and speak correctly. However, no research proves that grammar will "work" for this purpose. In 1963, Braddock, Lloyd-Jones, and Schoer examined all the earlier studies on the subject and concluded that "the teaching of formal grammar has a negligible or, because it usually displaces some instruction and practice in actual composition, even a harmful effect on the improvement of writing." [1]

All later research has supported this judgment, yet the public continues to clamor for grammar. We English teachers cannot ignore this overriding social fact but must deal with it intelligently. My "future grammar" does exactly that. It does not deny the importance of rules and standards, but it broadens the concept of grammar beyond the mere memorizing of facts and principles into a creative exploration of our language.

Students begin to understand that the English language is an organized set of symbols by which we mutually communicate in speech and writing. When we use this system of symbols, we demonstrate our humanity: No other living beings use language as we do. It helps us think, experience, and aspire. It unifies our society and underlies all our literature. It is our most precious treasure and our strong source of comfort and power. Future grammar considers language broadly from all these points of view.

Future grammar centers first on a small set of grammatical concepts along with the vocabulary for talking about them. Separated from

---

[1] *Research in Written Composition*, NCTE, Urbana, Ill., 1963, pp. 37–38.

the usual discussions of correctness, these concepts are easily learned. The key concepts are the following:

1. The four basic parts of speech—*noun, verb, adjective, adverb*—plus the function words that are married to them—*determiners* and *prepositions* to nouns, *auxiliaries* to verbs, *intensifiers* to adjectives and adverbs.
2. The sentence viewed as a two-part pattern, the two parts being subject and predicate, within which the parts of speech take their meaning from the context.
3. The *singulary* transformations, by which any sentence can be changed to a question, a negative, a command, or another related structure.
4. The *joining* transformation, which uses *and* plus a few other conjunctions to combine items of equal grammatical weight, thus creating compound sentences and structures.
5. The *inserting* transformations, which create complex sentences by inserting subordinate clauses into main clauses and into other subordinate clauses.

We can pleasantly teach and students can effectively learn these basic concepts by studying literature and composition with the help of the following twenty linguistic questions. In planning teaching strategy, we select and adapt questions relevant to the writing being studied, to our own teaching goals, and to the students in the class. These twenty questions follow, each briefly explained. Then relevant ones are applied to a selection from a short story to demonstrate how a teacher might adapt them in teaching this material to secondary students.

LINGUISTIC QUESTIONS [2]

1.   **What are the unusual words, and what do they mean in this context? What other meanings for them do you know? What synonyms could be substituted for them in this context?**

Words often have more than one meaning. Students may know one meaning and that one may not be correct for the context. A thesaurus may tempt students to use new synonyms unwisely. We need to locate and explain problem words in students' reading and writing.

---

[2] The linguistic questions are listed and explained in Malmstrom, Jean, *Understanding Language: A Primer for the Language Arts Teacher*, St. Martin's Press, New York, 1977, pp. 103–110. They are also applied to five literary selections, pp. 110–130.

2.   **What part of speech is this word in this context? What other part(s) of speech can it be in other contexts?**

A word's part of speech depends on its use in a sentence. Many words can be more than one part of speech. Take *round,* for example.

As a *noun:* Gary played a round of golf.
As a *verb:* Did the car round the corner on two wheels?
As an *adjective:* Joel bought a round box.
As a *preposition:* We jogged round the track.

In reading, if students misjudge a word's part of speech, they miss the meaning. In writing, when students realize that words are so flexible, they use them more intelligently.

3.   **What is the proportion of long to short words? How does it affect the difficulty of the selection?**

Long words can be arbitrarily defined as those of three or more syllables. In reading, too many long words intimidate students. In writing, too many long words may create an inappropriately pretentious tone.

4.   **What is the author's policy about repeating words as contrasted with using a variety of synonyms? What are the advantages and/or disadvantages of repetition?**

Many authors deliberately repeat words instead of using a variety of synonyms. They may wish to emphasize the word or play on its sound, for example. Accidental, meaningless repetition is rare in literature, but frequent in student writing. We can explain the virtues of meaningful repetition and the vices of random, pointless repetition.

5.   **If the author uses intensifiers, how does this use strengthen or weaken the selection?**

Intensifiers are a special group of adverbials that modify adjectives and adverbs but not verbs. *Very* is the most common intensifier. If it is overused, it loses its force. In judging the effectiveness of intensifiers, we guess the reasons for using them and then judge the value of those reasons.

6.   **Which words cluster into collocations to emphasize various ideas in the selection?**

Collocations are groups of related words that occur close together in a literary selection and reinforce the idea or meaning around which they cluster. For example, a collocation about spring includes *April, bud, fresh, grow, shower, sunshine, mud, warm, wet* and many other words.

7.   What is the proportion of factual to evaluative adjectives? How does it affect the tone of the selection?

Factual adjectives refer to facts that can be perceived by the five senses—*green, cold, wet*—whereas evaluative adjectives express opinions or value judgments—*good, lovely, wonderful*. Of course, many adjectives are hard to classify—*old, hard, tall*. The quality of adjectives is an important part of tone in literature and composition.

8.   What comparisons are there? Are any of them clichés? How do the comparisons strengthen or weaken the selection?

Worn-out comparisons are clichés. They have been so overused that they have lost their originality. However, an adult's cliché may be new and vivid to a child. It is better to discuss the accuracy of the comparison rather than its novelty.

9.   How frequent are regional and/or social dialect markers? What reasons does the author have for using dialect and how valid are those reasons?

Authors often bring their characters to life by having them use dialect words, structures, and pronunciations. If the dialect enhances the characterizations, it serves a valid purpose. However, dialect can easily be overdone, and then it can make the writing hard to read and understand.

10.   What complications are caused by the historical development of our language?

Words change constantly in meaning. Slang dates especially fast. In reading literature, students may be puzzled by old-fashioned words and meanings. Even words that do not seem old-fashioned to us teachers may confuse students and need explanation. On the other hand, students' supermodern slang may confuse us.

11.   How frequent is the definite article "the" as opposed to the indefinite article "a" ("an")? How does this frequency reflect the author's relationship to the reader?

The and *a* (*an*) are determiners and signal "noun coming up." *The* is the definite article and *a* and *an* are indefinite articles. The frequent use of *the* seems to imply that the author is close to the reader and seems to be saying, "You know what I mean. We understand each other." For example, in "The Star-Spangled Banner," the frequency of *the* suggests that the author and the reader are united in their knowledge and feelings about "the land of the free and the home of the brave." If such intimacy is true and intended, the use of *the* enhances it and is effective. Otherwise, it is not. Readers and writers decide.

12.   **What is the distribution of sentence types: fragments, basic sentences (with or without singulary transformations), sentences with joining transforms, inserting transforms, or both? How does this distribution affect the reading ease or difficulty of the selection?**

In their speech, students use all types of transformations, but in reading and writing, overly complex sentences cause problems in comprehension. On the other hand, if students' written sentences are monotonously simple, sentence-combining practice enhances their syntactic maturity. Any composition is a potential exercise in sentence combining.

13.   **How frequent are imperatives with and/or without "you" expressed? What reasons may explain the imperatives in this context?**

In using imperatives, a writer is speaking directly to the reader, thus creating a face-to-face intimacy between them. Discussing imperatives highlights their appropriateness or inappropriateness in the context.

14.   **If the word order is inverted, how can it be rearranged into normal modern English? What reasons may explain the inversion and how valid are those reasons?**

Normal word order in modern English sentences is subject–verb–object. Any other order may confuse students, and yet other orders are common in poetry for rhyme and rhythm and also in prose—usually for emphasis. We need to straighten out unusual word order so that it does not confuse students.

15.   **How can a change in intonation change the meaning of a particular word or sentence in the selection?**

Stress, pitch, and pause are important signals of meaning in English speech. We can pronounce any sentence in many ways, and each change affects its meaning. Students can explore possibilities, experimenting with various intonations, as they read literature and their own writing aloud.

16.   **How powerfully do verbs carry meaning without adjectives or manner adverbs to help them?**

Strong writing is often marked by vivid verbs instead of weak verbs plus helper adjectives or adverbs: *obey* instead of *be obedient, apologize* instead of *be apologetic, yell* instead of *speak loudly, grip* instead of *hold firmly.* Recognizing powerful verbs increases students' understanding of literature and encourages them to seek strong verbs in their own writing.

17.   What peculiarities in spelling or punctuation are present? How can they be explained?

In literature, unusual spellings may be archaic, as in the King James Bible, or regionally dialectal as in *The Jack Tales,* or both regionally and socially dialectal as in Joel Chandler Harris's Uncle Remus stories. Unusual punctuation may be old-fashioned, as in *Grimm's Fairy Tales,* or meaningfully individualistic as in the poetry of e. e. cummings. Such facts highlight contrasts and add interest to the study of spelling and punctuation.

18.   How does the author use sounds in the literary selection?

Students are normally aware of how sounds enhance effects in literature as in music. They can then be encouraged to try for some of the same effects in their own writing.

19.   How does the author use rhythm in the literary selection?

Students normally have a well-developed sense of rhythm and can easily appreciate the rhythms of literature. Understanding how professional writers use rhythm helps students to imitate this device.

20.   In analyzing a poem, what tension, if any, can be found between the rhythms of normal speech and the metrical patterns of the poem?

Normal English intonation has at least three contrasting degrees of stress or emphasis. Classical metrical analysis has only two degrees of stress—long and short, or strong and weak. This three-to-two mismatch causes interesting tension. In order to read poetry well, the reader must avoid a singsong beat on the one hand and unstructured prose rhythm on the other.

To demonstrate how a teacher might select and apply linguistic questions, I have chosen a few paragraphs from Harlan Ellison's " 'Repent, Harlequin!' Said the Ticktockman." [3] Ellison is concerned about the effects of modern technology on human beings. In this story, people have become so obsessed with punctuality that lateness is a crime punish-

---

[3] From *The Hugo Winners,* Isaac Asimov, ed., Doubleday, Garden City, N.Y., 1971, p. 480. I am grateful to my student, Martha Kirk, who first called the story to my attention.

able by the subtraction of each late minute from the tardy person's life. This time-bound society is personified by the Ticktockman, or Master Timekeeper, one of the two main characters in the story. The other is Harlequin, a nonconformist, who wears motley and bells, and who is unpredictable and rather childish. He has just dumped $150,000 worth of jelly beans from his air car on the shift-changing traffic below.

Jelly beans! Millions and billions of purples and yellows and greens and licorice and grape and raspberry and mint and round and smooth and crunchy outside and soft-mealy inside and sugary and bouncing jouncing tumbling clittering clattering skittering fell on the heads and shoulders and hard-hats and carapaces of the Timkin workers, tinkling on the slidewalk and bouncing away and rolling about underfoot and filling the sky on their way down with all the colors of joy and childhood and holidays, coming down in a steady rain, a solid wash, a torrent of color and sweetness out of the sky from above, and entering a universe of sanity and metronomic order with quite-mad coocoo newness. Jelly beans!

The shift workers howled and laughed and were pelted, and broke ranks, and the jelly beans managed to work their way into the mechanism of the slidewalks after which there was a hideous scraping as the sound of a million fingernails rasped down a quarter of a million blackboards, followed by a coughing and a sputtering, and then the slidewalks all stopped and everyone was dumped thisawayandthataway in a jackstraw tumble, and still laughing and popping little jelly beans eggs of childish color into their mouths. It was a holiday, and a jollity, and an absolute insanity, a giggle. But . . .

The shift was delayed seven minutes.

They did not get home for seven minutes.

The master schedule was thrown off by seven minutes.

Quotas were delayed by inoperative slidewalks for seven minutes.

TEACHING GOALS

In choosing this selection for exploring grammar through literature, the teacher might have the following teaching goals in mind. These goals determine the choice of linguistic questions.

1. To demonstrate that long sentences are not necessarily difficult sentences. Grammar, not length, determines sentence difficulty.

2. To demonstrate how English creates compound words.
3. To analyze how the grammar of literature can intensify its impact and enhance its meaning.
4. To show how word choice reinforces tone in literature.

To reach these goals, the teacher could select linguistic questions 1, 4, 6, 7, 8, and 12.

Linguistic question 1 calls attention to the following unusual words: *carapaces* (hard protective shields guarding the back), *metronomic* (mechanically regular in time, as if measured by a metronome), *inoperative* (out of order). Other unusual words are interesting examples of English word-building techniques: *soft-mealy, quite-mad, thisawayandthataway.*

Linguistic question 4 highlights the repetition of words and phrases: *and* (31 times), *the* and *a* (*an*) (14 times each), *jelly bean, seven minutes,* and *slidewalks* (4 times each), *laugh* and *work* (twice each).

Lingustic question 6 reveals at least two important contrasting collocations: a *happy-childhood collocation* containing such words as *jelly beans, holidays jackstraw, jollity, giggle, bouncing, jouncing,* and *tumbling;* and a *dehumanized-adulthood collocation* containing such words as *hard-hats, carapaces, workers, metronomic, mechanized, master schedule,* and *inoperative.* There are also color and taste collocations, both characteristic of the joys of childhood.

Linguistic question 7 focuses on the adjectives of the selection. Only *hideous* is an evaluative adjective; all the other adjectives are factual: *round, smooth, crunchy, soft-mealy, sugary, steady, solid, metronomic, quite-mad, coocoo, little, childish,* and *inoperative.*

Lingustic question 8 looks at the comparisons in the selection, none of which is a cliché. Two particularly interesting ones are *a steady rain, a solid wash, a torrent of color and sweetness out of the sky* and *hideous scraping as the sound of a million fingernails rasped down a quarter of a million blackboards.*

Linguistic question 12 examines sentence types in the selection. There are two fragments: *Jelly beans!* (twice). There are no basic sentences. All the sentences except the last four have both joining and inserting transformations. Joining transformations are especially apparent because of the high frequency of the conjunction *and.* The last four sentences have no joining transformations but show three passives: *was delayed, was thrown off,* and *were delayed.*

Having noted these linguistic, grammatical facts, the teacher is ready to prepare a teaching plan that will capitalize on them to achieve the desired teaching goals.

TEACHING PLAN

After the students have read the entire Ellison story, the teacher can open the discussion by rereading the selection aloud and defining the hard words like *carapaces, metronomic,* and *inoperative.* Talk can then move to Ellison's made-up words like *soft-mealy, quite-mad, slidewalks,* and *thisawayandthataway,* which combine familiar words to make new compounds to create vivid pictures in the reader's mind. Students can experiment with making up such new words of their own.

Further discussion can elicit the two key collocations of *happy childhood* and *dehumanized adulthood,* which clarify the contrast between Harlequin's joyous jelly beans and the Ticktockman's strict workaday world. Students observe that Ellison prefers joy to routine because his happy words far outnumber his stern ones. Indeed, joy predominates in the first two paragraphs, which jointly contain 214 words. The remaining four sentences, with a total of only thirty-two words, report the depressing results of breaking the rules of the dehumanized adult society. Students can inspect their own writing to note their uses of collocations and emphasis by reiteration.

Within each part of the selection, the grammar further reinforces Ellison's contrast between joyous childhood and grim adulthood. In the first two paragraphs, students can count the number of *and*s while observing how their frequency reflects the language of young children, who often "string ideas together with *and*" to make long sentences. These sentences are not usually hard to understand, however. Nor are Ellison's long sentences difficult. Contrariwise, the grammar of the last four sentences is not childish. They read like a formal report. They use no *and*s, but they have three passive transforms with the actors' names deleted. The impersonal tone is characteristic of report language, as students are probably aware. The repetition of the time adverbial *seven minutes* asserts the cruciality of time. Such words as *shift, schedule,* and *quota* reiterate that importance. Students can experiment with telling another story in child language and in report language to underline these uses of grammar.

A discussion of the adjectives in the selection may well lead to the general conclusion that all of them except *hideous* are factual. We can only guess about Ellison's reasons for his choices. Students will offer various suggestions. Certainly, factual adjectives are appropriate to the mechanized society of the Ticktockman, which is more concerned with facts than opinions. On the other hand, factual adjectives are equally appropriate to the world of Harlequin, but for a different reason. They assert that the "quite-mad coocoo newness" is also an observable fact. Students may offer other reasons and should be encouraged to do so.

Examination of Ellison's figurative language can lead to other open-ended discussion. In the first paragraph, the falling jelly beans are compared to *a steady rain, a solid wash, a torrent of color and sweetness out of the sky.* . . . This metaphor emphasizes the reality of Harlequin's world, since it is like the real world of the reader where liquid rain falls. In the second paragraph, the words *a hideous scraping as the sound of a million fingernails rasped down a quarter of a million blackboards* offer another real-world comparison. We recognize and shudder at the remembered sound. Thus, Ellison's comparisons assert that Harlequin's world is as real as the world of the Ticktockman. Students may discover other figurative language in the selection that further reinforces this point. They may also invent their own substitute comparisons and observe how these affect the meanings of the selection.

In all discussions of literature, and in all subsequent writing activities growing from these discussions, the teacher encourages students to develop their own opinions. Although the teacher's ideas are undoubtedly more informed and mature, they should not control or limit the discussions of the literature or the related composition activities. Students need freedom of opinion and expression to become truly involved with future grammar in literature and writing. Linguistic questions interestingly force their attention to the grammar of language in action in order to inform their opinions and reactions.

Future grammar itself is not really new. The parts of speech are the same, the sentence structures are the same, the techniques of analysis are the same. But instead of focusing exclusively on making children "talk right," future grammar places stress on helping them understand the full play of language in literature and in their own writing. No dramatic revolution is required to bring future grammar about. All we need is here now in our children and in the literature and composition we teach.

Talkin' and Testifyin'
About Black Dialect:
Past, Present, and Future Tense[1]

GENEVA SMITHERMAN

First off, we got to start with some basics. This gon be a article bout the language aspect of English teaching. Since black idiom is the "dialect of my nurture," and since I believe in the legitimacy of all dialects of American English, uhm gon run it down in the black thang. Course this ain gon be totally possible due to the limitations of print media, but uhm gon be steady tryin. This ain no long way from English teachin, cause uhm gon run down now some points bout inhumane language attitudes in our distant and not too distant past before goin on to speculate bout the future. Y'all follow me now cause it gon get deep.

PAST TENSE

Though most of the recent hullabaloo on dialects done focused on black speech, a social dimension interacts with the racial factor, throwing standard versus nonstandard English into a wider realm that affects whites also. What linguist Donald Lloyd called the "national mania for correctness" stems from a long-standing tradition of elitism in American life and language matters. Although Americans preach individualism and class mobility, they practice conformity and class stasis. Further, those folk on the lower rung of the socioeconomic ladder, in their upwardly mobile, catch-up-with-the Joneses efforts, become unwitting accomplices in their own linguistic and cultural demise.

---

[1] Adapted from "Soul 'N Style," a column appearing in *The English Journal*, February, March, April, and May, 1974. Reprinted by permission of the publisher, The National Council of Teachers of English.

Reflecting this class anxiety (neurosis?), schoolroom grammars are grounded in the "doctrine of correctness" that emerged during the eighteenth century and was coincident with the rise of the so-called primitive middle classes and the decline of the mythical "refined" aristocracy (those same "high-class" folk, mind you, whose greed both led to wars over land and property and initiated the slave trade). In determining educational policy for the middle class, the power elite decided that the kids should be instructed in their vernacular, the Anglo-Saxon tongue, since their "lowly" origins indicated that they could not possibly master Latin, which had been the lingo of instruction for the elite.

Now in those days, English was considered quite disorderly and god-awfully discordant with Latin rules. Moreover, the fresh-from-the-bottom middle-class speakers of English wanted neither themselves nor they kids to reflect any kinship with those they left behind. Therefore, early English grammarians sought to regularize and "purify" English speech by superimposing upon it the "prestigious" Latinate grammatical model, like the good Bishop Robert Lowth, who conceptualized his grammar in terms of giving what he called "order and permanence to the unruly, barbarous tongue of the Anglo-Saxons" (*Short Introduction to English Grammar,* 1763).

The killin part bout the whole mess, though, is there's little correspondence between the two languages! For instance, dig on the fact that in Latin you really can't end sentences with prepositions cause Latin prepositions are attached to the verb, prefix-style, but in English, prepositions are movable. Hence, Latin *de*voro for English swallow *down*—i.e., in the sense of *put up with.* (Y'all know my man Winston Churchill's thang on this, don't you: "This is the kind of nonsense up with which I will not put." Git it, Winston!)

Americans fought a war to sever they colonial ties, but these British-based language attitudes came right on cross the water. Lowth's American counterparts are dudes like Lindley Murray and Goold Brown.

In the twentieth century, the individual, Latinate-based norms were replaced by social group and ethnicity-based norms. Structuralist grammarians studied English in action and revealed that "socially acceptable" and highly educated types were making all sorts of departures from Latinate rules, like saying "It is me." Consequently, the definition of "standard" English shifted to "the type of English used by the socially acceptable of most of our communities" (Charles Fries, *American English Grammar,* 1940, in his recommendation to public school teachers). Instead of freeing speakers and writers from petty and elitist linguistic amenities, the immediate educational application of structuralist research was toward linguistic and social conformity for the children whose parents had immigrated to this country in massive numbers around the turn of the century. "No broken English in this class, Antonio," and so on like that.

Dig where uhm comin from: This new "standard" didn't make thangs no better for common folk, nor for so-called "divergent" speakers. It wasn't never no meltin pot. As Don Lee has said, it melted, and we blacks burned. In the process, so did a lot of other beautiful, "divergent" languages and cultures. Cause the immigrants' kids became ashamed of they mommas and daddies, who had sweated and toiled to bring 'they families to this country and then turned around and sweated some more to send they kids to school only to find those kids embarrassed about them and they speech.

Now teachers in general, but English teachers in particular, got to take some of this weight, cause they bees steady intimidatin kids bout they "incorrect English." Yet this superimposition of a polite usage norm has *nothin* to do with linguistic versatility, variety of expression, and the "power of the rap," but *everythin* to do with the goal of cultural and linguistic eradication by making what one seventeenth-century grammarian called the "depraved language of common people" and, by extension, the common people themselves conform to the dominant (white, middle-class) ethic of the new aristocracy.

Hey, why don't y'all cool it, cause that sho ain humane.

PRESENT TENSE

American educational institutions is continuing they role as passive reflectors of a racist, inhumane society. In part, the contemporary madness bees manifest in the "language deprivation" teaching strategies for the "disadvantaged" black American. Suddenly!!!!! after more than three centuries on this continent, the educational and societal consensus is that Blacks have a "language problem." But wasn't nobody complainin bout black speech in 1619 when the first cargo of Africans was brought to Colonial America. Nor in 1719, 1819, 1919—really, it wasn't till bout the 1950s when it became evident that Afros was really beginning to make some economic headway in America that everybody and they momma started talkin bout we didn talk right. (It was bout that time—1956 to be exact—that yours truly was a college freshman forced to enroll in speech *therapy*—uh-huh, you heard me—cause of my "regional"—now they just say "black"—dialect.)

In the current controversy surrounding black speech (as well as other so-called "minority" dialects) linguists/educators/English teachers and just plain folk bees comin from one of three bags: (1) eradicationist; (2) bi-dialectalist; (3) legitimizer. These positions have undergirding them not simply linguistic issues but important sociopolitical concerns. (I mean, where is yo head?) While Ima rap specifically bout the black thang, with minor modifications, what Ima say can apply to most "divergent" dialects. (Now I ain gon cite no specific folk, since this piece ain bout name-callin. But once upon a time, I did this. See my "The Black Idiom in White Institutions," *Negro American Literature Forum,* Fall, 1971.)

Eradicationist

Now this is a old position and don't too many people hold it no more, since it ain considered cool (if you black) or liberal (if you white) to be one. Essentially, they say get rid of the dialect; it's illogical, sloppy, and underdeveloped. It retards reading ability and the acquisition of language skills and thus is dysfunctional in school. It is the language of Uncle Tom and thus is dysfunctional in the socioeconomic world. Ergo, the only way to facilitate the up-from-the-ghetto rise of black folk is to obliterate what one educator deemed "this last barrier to integration." (Couldn't resist that one!)

Bi-dialectalist

Not so, say these holders of the most popularly prevailing position. Linguistic analysis demonstrates that the dialect is perfectly systematic and capable of generating cognitive concepts. Blacks acquire language at the same rate and with the same degree of fluency as whites. Because Blacks learn they language patterns in a black environment, they manifest they linguistic competence in black English whereas whites do it in white English. And if reading teachers is hip to the phonological system of black speech, then there ain no reading problem. However, there do be that social/real (?) world out there. And Blacks will need to acquire the "prestige" usage system in order to facilitate they socioeconomic mobility. At the same time, bi-dialectalists recognize that Blacks need they powerful and efficient dialect to function/survive in they own communities. So the solution is for Blacks to be bi-dialectal.

Legitimizer

Now enterin the lists is a small but highly vocal group who bees contendin that while the former group is linguistically inaccurate and outright racist, the latter is politically naive and pedagogically wrongheaded. After all, if the dialect is not the problem, but sociolinguistic attitudes are, then why not work to change those attitudes? While we may be talkin bout Blacks enterin the mainstream, we can change the course of that stream. Not *can* but *is*—since black language (as well as other black cultural patterns) is rapidly being adopted by whites. Not *can* but *got to*—since cultural plurality don't mean remake black folk in white face. Anyway, if racism persists, all the language education in the world won't help you.

It is simply hypocritical to tell kids that they lingo is cool in the home environment, but not in school and mainstream America. (That's how come Black folk bees so schizophrenic-seemin, all time havin to front and mask, go through linguistic and other kind of changes round whites.) Kids say don't run that game on me bout it's good enough for the ghetto but not the suburbs. Like everybody know the suburbs represent money and success, so who want anythang associated with the opposite? Eventually then, black bi-dialectalists become mono-dialectalists cut off from those they left behind. Moreover, the way this country is presently constituted, there ain enough jobs for *nobody,* don't care how well they can manipulate *s*'es and *ed*'s in they speech. Thus, bi-dialectalism is not based on a sophisticated analysis of American power relations.

We legitimizers query: Why waste valuable school time on polite usage drills when, in a sense, black kids is already bi-dialectal? Due to mass media, and after a few years in school, they understand white English and can produce reasonable facsimiles. Witness a group of black kids "playin white." (Remember that scene from *Native Son?*) Listen to them, and you will hear the most amazing (amazing to the unhip, that is) mimicking of white folks' language you ever heard. Or get on the bus and check out a group of domestics on they way home talkin bout and linguistically imitatin Miss Ann. I mean, they bees doin a pretty good (i.e., accurate) job of it.

Bi-dialectal classroom approaches and drills are all the more pointless when we note the few currently remaining deep structure differences between these two closely related dialects of American English. Bi-dialectalists note this too, and some done admirably demonstrated it through linguistic analysis. Yet, ironically, they persist in devising and teaching materials stressing these superfluous features of English usage. (I told y'all in the beginning this was all bout madness, didn't I?) For instance, the kid who wonders what's the difference between what I wrote —"he do"—and your correction—"he does"—is really posing a linguistically legitimate question, since there ain no deep structure—underlyin semantic differentiation—between the two. As a matter of fact, many features of black English grammatical structure, which teachers bees so uptight bout, is simply surface features of English, differing in "flavoring but not in substance." Thus, *Ain nobody doin nothin* is merely another surface representation of *Nobody is doing anything; I seen him, I saw him; They lost they books* is the same as *They lost their books.* And so on.

Speaking to the legitimacy of minority dialects in the English classroom do not mean abdication of responsible language teaching. It do not mean lettin kids get away with irresponsible, disorganized uses of language and communication. Righteous teachers taking care of business in the English classroom must see to it that kids learn to compose coherent, documented, specific, logical—in short, rhetorically powerful oral and/or written communications. There's good rappers and there's bad rappers, and anythang do not go in the black community, just as anything does not go in the white community. Uhm talkin bout redefinin what *do* go. And it mean more than zeroin in on usage, on such trivia as movin students from *they house* to *their house*. This is an abdication of responsibility, for that's only a lateral move, and like my man Curtis Mayfield sing, we got to keep movin on up—*up,* not sideways.

In movin up, however, we must be careful to sustain our moral-ethical vision of the universe and, if necessary, choose goodness over grammar. As Jess B. Simple says:

> If I get the sense right . . . the grammar can take care of itself. There are plenty of Jim Crowers who speak grammar, but do evil. I have not had enough schooling to put words together right—but I know some white folks who have went to school forty years and do not DO right. I figure it is better to do right than to write right, is it not? [2]

FUTURE TENSE

If y'all been following me, by now you's bound to be wonderin: Where do we go from here? Let me suggest some "places."

First and most important is the reading problem in black schools that crops up in all areas. Kids fail social studies and science classes cause they can't read the text; in math, they can't understand the story problems; they love gym and drivers' training, but they have trouble with the health ed manuals and the written tests for drivers; girls in sewing classes can't read the pattern instructions, and so on—every school subject as well as survival in the larger society depends on ability to read. Research has shown that, ironically, the longer black kids stay in school, the further behind they get—e.g., if they reading level is two years behind at grade five, it'll be about four years behind at grade ten.

Now, don't get shook, I ain gon say (as some blacks have indeed advocated) that black kids oughta drop out of school altogether—I knows better, cause ain *nothin* on the streets but trouble. Nor am I gon say, as some whites have, that schools failed, after all, cause schools spent all

---

[2] Hughes, Langston, *Simple Stakes a Claim.* See my "Grammar and Goodness," *English Journal,* May 1973, for the full quote.

that cash doing more of the same thangs they'd done wrong in the past; the instructional forms were different but the underlying ideology was the same. For example, due to hang-ups about black English, some school systems invested much time, effort, and money in language change programs and in dialect readers, some even going so far as making kids plod through two versions of the same story, one in so-called "home" dialect, the other in "school" dialect. Yet the only dialect "interference" in communication and in the learning-to-read process is the teacher's inability (or unwillingness?) to accept the black kid's dialect.

Dig on the fact that before about 1950, most black folks going through the educational system learned reading and communication skills, despite speaking the black tongue. This same dialect has only in the last twenty years or so "interfered" with the learning process, owing on the one hand to white fear of the rapid socioeconomic advancement of Blacks during the 1940s and 1950s and on the other, to the blackenization of American cities. As urban areas and subsequently their schools became blacker, whites fled to the suburbs. Although the teachers continued to work in city schools, they no longer lived in the environment. (I remember my days in a lower East Side Detroit elementary school in 1947 when several of my teachers lived within a 10 to 12 block radius of our school.) Thus, these teachers as well as the generation after them became vastly alienated from black language and culture. In addition to the white teachers who don't know what's goin down with black language, there are black teachers who, being recent arrivals from the lower class themselves, reject the dialect as a stigmatized reminder of where they came from. (There may be some Blacks who are truly ignorant of the forms of the idiom, but there sho ain many. For more on black ambivalence toward black language, see Frantz Fanon, *Black Skins, White Masks*.)

Enter a black kid reading the sentence, *"The boy needs more money,"* as *"De boy need mow money."* All he has done is deleted the final *r* in *more*, the *s* in the third person verb, and substituted *d* for initial *th* in *the*. Teachers hip to the system of black pronunciation patterns know that obviously such a kid does not have either a perceptual/vision problem or a coding/decoding linguistic one—he has simply "translated" the sentence on the printed page into good black English. Doing this often produces homophonic pairs like: *then/den* (initial *th* pronounced as *d*); *more/mow, four/foe, during/doing, Paris/pass, sore/so* (due to intervocalic and final *r* not being pronounced); *sing/sang, ring/rang* (vowel i + nasal ng = æ + ng). If this seems odd, recall that there are homophones in white middle class dialect, like *here/hear; their/ they're/there*. It's simply that black English speakers have some additional and/or different sets of homophones. With this kind of knowledge and acceptance of black English in mind, language arts teachers can push on toward increasing the black kid's cognitive command of reading materials—and do so with the regular basal reading material, which represents, after all, the functional dialect of newspapers, street signs, application forms, and most of what they'll have to read outside of school. (For research in this reading-dialect area that supports what I'm runnin down here, see the works of William Labov and of Kenneth Goodman and the articles in *Teaching Black Children to Read.*)

On the secondary level, English teachers should put aside the diagramming exercises (yeah, I done recently seen teachers *still* doing this!), postpone the transformational grammar lessons, and more profitably sail full-speed ahead on a real need: functional literacy. Get out the reading kits, set up reading labs, design remedial reading programs, and, if necessary, concentrate *all* classroom time on this excruciating problem. (You can still even teach literature this way; just make each lesson in literature a reading lesson also.) Especially on this level, students should be learning to comprehend the structure and language of what I call *social negotiation forms*—marks of this highly bureaucratic society we live in, such as forms for health insurance, job applications, voter registration, social security, driver's license, college entrance, Medicare, etc.

Another "place" to go is to the media. We live in a multimedia world where most of our important and even complex information and ideas are acquired and transmitted through audio-oral-visual processes. Help students critically examine various media, noting how visual arrangement, selection of material, style of presentation, and the like all help to color our perceptions of reality and convey hidden messages. (For example, until recently, black ad models were all high-yellows with straight hair.) Students should be encouraged to evaluate and develop standards of excellence for television programs and films. A quick glance at the recent (t)rash of black exploitation films makes this an absolute necessity, and as for seeing black dudes like Shaft on the tube, if they ain gon be no more ethical and responsible than whites, then we've only substituted black trash for white.

While our society is such that basic literacy is still vital, professional writers and English majors aside, don't nobody else be needin to write. Thus, since students (both black and white) will do far more speaking than writing in life after school—this applies even to college graduates—the English classroom's conventional written tasks should give way to speech activities. Specific assignments might involve simulation routines, such as job interview situations, panel discussions, debates, improvisational drama, and so on. Needless to say, listening skills should be stressed as an important counterpart to speaking. Assessment of student products and follow-through teaching still applies because contrary to what is often said, anythang do not go in speech just as anything does not go in writing. Whether we're talking about Blacks or whites, even the most casual speech events have their norms and stylistic criteria, which—do it need sayin?—ain got nothin to do with dialect but with thangs like strategy of presentation.

If writing *is* taught, it should be used as a vehicle for teaching thought—logic, organization, critical thinking, and analysis. This approach to writing sees language as a way of organizing experience, and it emphasizes written composition as a process of discovery—often writing is a way of finding out what you think about a subject.

With this approach the question is: Does the paper communicate the writer's message? (Indeed, does it even have a message? Some of the papers written in even the most "whitest" English bees sometimes *pointless!*) Is the paper well-organized, logical? Are there facts and supporting details for the writer's ideas? Did he/she take his audience into account in selecting a suitable topic and in presenting the pertinent facts about the topic? Thus, traditional notions of mechanical correctness become irrelevant, but the English teacher's job becomes harder, since red-penciling black English forms is really a faster and easier method of grading papers.

Whenever possible, work in some lessons on language and culture and social and regional dialects. Since English is the one school subject that everybody takes, and since people's language attitudes are fostered in the schools, you, the English teacher, can do a great deal to eradicate the nonsense about, and push for the acceptance of, all dialects in both white and black students. Dig it: Today's students will become the employment managers, businessmen, and social managers of tomorrow. Since "divergent dialects" have been used as a tool of oppression, refusing to accept the biases of the world "out there" and effectuating language attitude change constitute a route to the achievement of cultural pluralism and the American ideal. If schools are to be the leaders that they should be, rather than the followers that they have been, the task of bringing the American dream to fruition has to begin with the individual teacher in his/her individual setting. And it ain too far-fetched to talk bout the English/language arts teacher as an agent of social change, cause like I said, everybody and they momma pass through school, even if they don't stay too long. If English teachers would work to change attitudes about dialects, both in and, wherever possible, outside of school, it would be a major step in the direction of a humane social universe. What I've been urging you, the English teacher, to do amounts to an individual social and political act, which like charity, begins at home.

Y'all keep the faith.

Separate Peaces

PATRICIA W. FOX

If the pleasures of teaching have outweighed the problems of teaching, you're still in there fighting. You have overcome the occasional obstreperous child, outlandish directive, or outmoded material. You have done battle; you have parlayed for peace. So have I, but lately I have begun to worry about the balance of problems and pleasures, because the traditional peace treaties haven't been suiting me or the problems. The alternative solutions that I have compiled here come from raised voices in faculty lounges or from conspiratorial tones on hall duty posts. I invite you to test those solutions that suit your attitudes toward your problems. (A quick index of varying emotional states appears in parentheses after each numbered alternative.)

PROBLEM A: THE CAPTIVE CURRICULUM

Interference threatens the curriculum. Your department capitulated to the student demand for a course in Free Reading but rejected *Classic Comics* as approved texts. To forestall further parent forays, you have added "Students will be introduced to diagramming the sentence" as a departmental objective but will keep secret the time alloted to the objective. At the behest of the funded career education director you have suffered the invasion of resource people who expound on THE IMPORTANCE OF ENGLISH IN THE REAL WORLD, including the one who stressed (for an entire class period) *hand*writing to an auditorium full of senior high students. You have doubled the number of clinics that prepare students for the format of the SAT, despite the fact that students from your school improved twenty points in the Verbal last year, an accomplishment met with total silence from those who bellowed disapproval of a former ten-point drop.

Halt infiltration of the ranks! An alternative can vanquish the enemies.

Alternative 1 (Modestly Subversive)

Try a new battery of concessions. Pull two or three detailed 1962 (1952?) courses of study from the mothballs. Using these as models, substitute new books and new objectives to sketch outlines for every new course suggestion from every complaining source. Simultaneously submit a stack of these proposals (the more the better) to the Student Council, to the Board of Education, and to the parent group to Save Our Schools. Include the State Board of Education's current fair-haired children such as the present Vocational and Careers Development Committee. Suggest that each group determine which four courses should be those required for graduation. The resulting internecine warfare will buy you time to concentrate on constructive curriculum change.

Alternative 2 (Evasive)

Guesstimate the *maximum* increase in staff and dollars to implement the new misdirected courses. Itemize the cost of optional kits, including tapes, transparencies, slides, reproducible dittos, and consumable student planning pads with attached magic markers. Throw in the former and current prices of paper clips. Offer your "facts" to the school district's loudest balanced-budget buff. He may buy you even more time than you'll really want.

Alternative 3 (Stuff-y)

Collect all suggestions—*must* English skills (like mnemonic devices for good listening), *mandatory* English materials (like Ph.D. level articles on last week's findings in DNA molecule research), and *relevant* relationships between English and all other disciplines (like the artistic arrangement, the errorless typing, and the proper grammar in the letter of complaint)—and *stuff* them into an existing course, any course. Publish copies of the course description. (Ditto is tacky. Mimeograph will do. Print requires administrative co-conspiracy or pretentious naiveté.) Distribute the copies—in whatever form—to the former critics as indisputable evidence that their suggestions have been put into practice. Then work on your own battle plan.

Alternative 4 (Liberal)

Plant in a list of possible new courses one of these titles: "Sex Roles in Drama," "Modern Marxist Novelists," "Gay Authors," or "The Beauty of Human Reproduction as Seen through Literature." It won't be necessary to publish the list anywhere. The next Board of Education meeting will be miraculously invaded with wild-eyed censors who will halt *all* curriculum change while they harangue everyone about impressionable children and the sanctity of the home. They will also probably attempt to discover the dirty communists behind the courses. Smile innocently.

Alternative 5 (Traditional)

Form a committee.

Alternative 6 (Progressive)

Propose that the committee be abolished, since it serves no useful function.

Alternative 7 (Grandiose)

If you have not completed your own plan for curriculum change, the Headquarters Command has reared its ugly head and has begun the Comprehensive Survey. Instead of informal questioning during staff meetings, the HQC dittos an opinionnaire and puts one in each teacher's mailbox; each is to be returned by Friday at 3 p.m. sharp! Instead of brainstorming with kids during classes, the HQC mimeographs a questionnaire that teachers will monitor during a special homeroom period next Tuesday which will make the bell schedule for the day the same as the Friday Pep Assembly Schedule except for early dismissal. Instead of chatting with parents on Back to School Nights, the Headquarters Command prints (remember about tacky ditto and not much better mimeo) a booklet of questions and mails 26,311 of them, one to each household in the community.

One school handles the Comprehensive Survey this way: After three rounds of reminders from the principal's secretary, 68 pecent of the staff opinionnaires are returned for her to tally. After salvaging 1,764 of the 1,901 questionnaires distributed to the students (116 were absent from school that day and 207 more were missing from the special questionnaire session), discarding the 391 blanks, and culling out the 69 basically obscene replies, teacher-monitors turn in replies from 58.5 percent of the 2,224-member student body. The Office Practice classes compile the results. Similar patterns pervade the schools in the rest of the district.

After postponing the official announcement twice (to make sure the slowness of the mails had not interfered), a Headquarters Command aide tells the local newspaper that they are "very pleased" with the 4,489 filled-in booklets that were mailed back in the stamped manila envelopes, and no, they haven't had time to figure the percentage of return. However, in at least one area the HQC "senses an overwhelming unanimity" among the three groups surveyed. The English Department can get started on curriculum changes, because each group surveyed considers reading and writing as critically important skills! No one else is available for comment.

PROBLEM B: THE NONCAPTIVATING CURRICULUM

A variation of Problem A prevails. You have met the enemy and he is you-all. Apathy abounds; the curriculum stagnates. Introductory English leads to Sophomore English which leads to Junior English which leads to the option of College Prep English or Practical English or no English.[1] Your colleagues haven't offered a new course since they put their wagons in a circle against some featherheaded attack. Enter featherheaded attack.

Alternative 1

OR·DER·LY (or' der lĭ) —adj. "characterized by an observance of order, rule, or discipline"; —n. "a person attending on a superior to carry order; an attendant charged with the maintenance of order, cleanliness, etc.")

The Department of Instruction outlines an orderly change. A Phase I study committee assesses "where we are," which shows everyone that we don't know where we are at all, because every English teacher from fourth through twelfth grades assumes the sole responsibility for introducing paragraphing. Undaunted, superiors launch orderlies into Phase II, "where we should be." Having taken two more years to assess, the Phase II orderlies report, but the DI scraps Phase III, "where we're gonna be." In the interim, a millage has failed or the superintendent has left. The Phase III structure, which the orderlies were to maintain and clean, bears the sign "Out of Order."

But never fear! The new superintendent has an orderly plan: Alpha Stage, the study of which will determine the student achievement in the cognitive and affective domains, will be followed by Beta Stage, which will relate the subordinate and superordinate structures to those domains, and be completed by Omega Stage, which becomes the latest fatality. In this interim, the federal funding well dried up, or a recall petition for half the Board was being circulated, or it is a negotiations year and the orderlies have been declared disorderly again.

---

[1] NB: Each student must be warned that the Principal's Recommendation [2] will not automatically accompany the student's transcript to an institution of higher learning if the student has not availed himself of the proper English option in his senior year.

[2] NBB: The Principal's Recommendation is not a requirement [3] of any of the institutions of higher learning but is evidence of a positive attitude and exemplary behavior on the part of any student receiving it.

[3] NNBB or NBBB: A requirement for graduation is evidence of an attempt to achieve the Principal's Recommendation, which, simply stated, every graduate gets.

As a foolhardy disorderly, perhaps you'll wear the white plume yourself. Try any of the following alternatives to apathy.

Alternative 2 (Surreptitious)

Hide your recent grad course in dialects in a thus extended unit of *Huck Finn*. Your enthusiasm will transcend both the student obliviousness to variety and the inappropriateness of the level of your material.

Alternative 3 (Stealthy)

Imbed transformational grammar concepts in the kids' battered *Handbook of English* texts between the Latin-based rules and the exercises with the answers already penciled in. Under no circumstances leave kernels or transforms around for any outsider to see.

Alternative 4 (Downright Furtive)

Graciously give up—for one turn—the shared class set of *Anthology of Literature through the Ages for Young People* and sneak camera-carrying students out of your classroom to create with film. Explain to the kids in advance that if they're caught, they're on their own, but if you're caught, they'll have to help bail you out, perhaps by demanding that your film unit become a full-fledged course. (Don't worry about the discrepancies in the advance arrangements. Kids who are suspended from school for skipping school are accustomed to illogic.)

Alternative 5 (Domino)

Send home a grade-warning notice for the daughter of a *VERY INFLUENTIAL PERSON* in the community who never messes around with pfc's and noncoms but goes straight to the top brass, so that the next morning the PRESIDENT OF THE SCHOOL BOARD calls the *Superintendent* who questions the Director of Instruction who challenges your principal who berates the asst. princ. of instr. who bawls out the English d. c. who not only chews you out but also calls a meeting of the whole department who must—before they go home that day—make curriculum changes to satisfy the *VERY INFLUENTIAL PERSON* in the community who doesn't care what changes are made as long as his daughter doesn't get any more grade-warning notices because she's bored with dull classes. Your department will be furious with you, so *mea culpa* it. Seek their forgiveness by volunteering to write up some curriculum changes in the name of the department. If your surreptitious, stealthy, or downright furtive changes have indeed gone unnoticed, your colleagues will allow you to do the work. If they're suspicious of your self-sacrifice, they'll offer their own changes. In either case, the department is out of the no-man's land of curriculum change.

PROBLEM C: THE OFFENSIVE TEXTBOOK

The armchair generals who consider themselves authorities on curriculum change become absolute experts with textbook selection. Since a textbook's accessibility makes it more vulnerable to attack than curriculum, many more battles are fought over books, often on fronts that have little to do with a book's instructional worth. Rarely do teachers find allies to help select a text. Usually teachers do battle with destructive censors rather than mere critics. Often teachers must defend themselves as well as their text selections. The following alternatives pertaining to the textbook offensive become strategies for survival.

Alternative 1 (Submissive)

Surrender.

Save your ammunition for a bigger fracas. When the foe storm the administration building over a book, it's usually a novel, a play, a collection of poetry—in short, literature being used as a text—and the charge usually is that it's a dirty book. Sometimes the wisest defense is retreat, especially when you know the great body of literature from which you can select again.

Alternative 2 (Incendiary)

When tempers flare over a book and the temperature on the outside has reached 451 degrees Fahrenheit, fight fire with fire. The alternatives can backfire (pun intended), but sometimes professional pride forces derring-do. Light a fire under the local civil liberties defenders. Informed, they'll attack the book burners and defend the right of free speech. The hazard is that it may take years in court during which time you won't have had the use of the book.

Start backfires with other professionals, getting ministers, doctors and dentists, college professors, lawyers and judges, and engineers to sign or to carry petitions supporting the book. The danger in that backfire is that *their* professional authority, not yours, has won the day, and you have swelled the ranks and the heads of "authorities" in education who are untrained, uncertified, and inexperienced except that they've been to a series of schools.

A final backfire possibility promises more backfire than solution, but it might be great fun to try. Offer alternative titles that will singe the eyebrows of the bookburners. If they object to *The Autobiography of*

Malcolm X, suggest the biography *The Happy Hooker.* Instead of *Slaughterhouse Five,* serve up *Breakfast of Champions.* Should they balk at *Catcher in the Rye,* toss them "Ball of Fat." If any hidden sense of proportion remains, everyone may have a good laugh and go back to work in his own specialty.

Chances are better that the conflagration will consume all.

Alternative 3 (Mata Harried)

Since forewarned is forearmed, infiltrate the meetings of the Minute Women—that's what they were actually called in our community —to discover what movie, TV or radio program, celebrity, or book is currently under attack. Discovering where and when they meet and wangling an invitation will be the easy steps. Sitting through endless meetings watching them salivate over the porno they would prevent will be somewhat more difficult, especially since you know that the material they gasp over has its major circulation within their group. As a card-carrying, clucking member, however, you will be watching for signs of a renewed attack on *Invisible Man, Grapes of Wrath,* or (and this one puzzles me yet) *The Good Earth.* When they begin drafting a position statement, woman the battle stations.

Alternative 4 (Imaginative)

Offer a study seminar through AAUW, the Delphian Society, an adult education class, a church study club, or any place that will have you. Title the class "What to Do about Dirty Books" and get the participants to read them from cover to cover, not turned-down page corner to turned-down page corner, making sure that they're books with substance between the turned-down corners. If this plan results in a truce, pass out copies of NCTE's *The Student's Right to Read* and let the new defenders make the next move.

Alternative 5 (Parentoid)

Knowing that a parent waving a book is lurking behind every tree and knowing that they are legion and you are only one, guard your flanks, cover your rear, and get help from above. For every book you select (or already have as a textbook) store ammunition from the quotations from *The English Journal,* the *Library Journal, Saturday Review,* and every educator or critic who says anything positive about the work or the author. Have the quotation-ammunition in reserve for the flank attack. Write your own defense of the book and why you have chosen it for students. Get others to sign it, including the brass and the president of the Minute Women. That's called covering your rear in advance.

Finally, get help from above. If you have ever ordered supplies through the army quartermaster corps or the Support Services of even a very small school system, your experience will help with a plot against future complaining parents. The procedures and forms to return the #564912 paper, construction, Golden Leaf yellow, $8\frac{1}{2} \times 11$, box, one, for the #564913 paper, construction, Golden Leaf yellow, $8\frac{1}{2} \times 14$, box, one, will adapt to the creation of an impenetrable maze of procedures and an insurmountable mountain of forms. Cap this by getting the final help from above. Get these Steps-to-Be-Followed-in-a-Parental-Complaint-of-a-Textbook made a **POLICY OF THE SCHOOL SYSTEM**. By the time a complaint gets to anyone who can do anything about it, the book will be out of print.

PROBLEM D: REVOLTING CIRCUMSTANCES

You've fought a delaying action with many of the self-proclaimed local authorities on curriculum and textbooks. (You hadn't really considered taking on submarine commanders or *Newsweek* editors.) You've jarred apathetic colleagues to some action. (You hadn't really considered taking on *student* apathy.) Lulled by the success of these skirmishes, you retreat to reverie. You remember when students didn't question your assignments or your motives or your credentials. Furthermore, you remember when their parents didn't. You remember when PTA/PTO meetings were tea and crumpets, not tar and feathers. You remember when the superintendent was Big Daddy, not Big Brother. You remember when kids' Friday afternoon chatter was about that night's sock hop, not its hash bash. You remember when an English teacher wasn't forced to fit in health education, sex education, career education, alternative education, global education, and values clarification education. You remember when businessmen minded their own businesses. You remember when education wasn't the scapegoat for all the ills of society. Remembering *when* triggers recognizing *now*. The real enemy, attitudinal change, has become thoroughly entrenched while we teachers sniped at shadows. Now to rout out the destructive attitudes we can use only militant methods.

Alternative 1 (Insurrectionist)

You needn't collect coke bottles, save rags, store cans of gasoline, or fill sandbags to be militant. A militant insurrectionist in education could line up testing policies as targets. It seems fitting. Since education has brainwashed everyone to accept a test as *the* tool of measurement, education should right its own wrong. Let's start by blowing the top off the SAT. Every school system in the nation should sign up extra "students" to take the test, the "students" being the teachers who monitor and the parents who pay. To publicize the always secret SAT questions, one parent at each testing site could make copies for later distribution and study. The teachers could go to work on the equally secret answers, each in his own expert field, identifying the multiple choices that were designed deliberately to mislead, pointing out the instances that offered more than one answer that could be "right," zeroing in on the flaws in the items that the test makers must have considered perfectly clear.

As an alternative to the alternative, what about having the top ten authors, university presidents, corporation presidents, congressmen, sports, TV, movie, and record stars, all the governors, and all the editors from *Newsweek* take the test? Let the flak fly where it may.

Having exploded the myth of the SAT, teachers could take on the state assessments. In Michigan, for example, it might be wise to alter some multiple-choice items on a fourth grade verbal test. Example: "An Indian lives in a (a) house, (b) fort, (c) cottage, (d) tepee." If you were a Michigan Indian, what would you answer? If you were a child who spent summers in a cottage near Walpole Island Indian Reservation, what would you answer? If you had absorbed all the TV stereotypes, what would you answer? If you were an Indian lore buff, what would you answer? If you were a test-item writer, what answer would you insist upon?

We could have at the standardized tests. For urban children perhaps we could alter one famous reading readiness test. We could begin by changing the item that pictures a rural-delivery mail box on a post, a picture that should be circled to go with the picture of the stamped letter. All city children must make this and many other "logical" connections to prove their readiness to read, despite the plethora of items which stem from rural origins.

Having straightened out the state and commercial interests, we should smoke out the local analysts of test scores, the ones who use identical statistics to prove opposite contentions, the ones who prove the old adage that figures don't lie but liars figure.

Alternative 2 (Revolutionary)

Damn the torpedoers! Blast the other ignorant authorities as well! Fire when you see the whites of their shirts! Be an army of dedicated (that's not new), determined (still not revolutionary), dissidents (now you're moving) who will openly challenge the management-by-objectives proponents who would run our schools like businesses, treating students like products to be rolled off assembly lines, treating teachers to time and motion studies, and treating school systems for fiscal ills only. Most of this militant activity will take place at Board of Education meetings.

Alternative 3 (Radical)

Radical alternatives are simply sensible ideas that weren't thought of by the people who have the authority/power to put them into practice. The following ideas seem very tame if you ignore the difficulty of putting each into practice and preface each with the phrase "Wouldn't it be nice if"—

- all prospective teachers were required to take at least one college course in writing.
- that course was taught by someone other than a teaching fellow.
- all literature teachers didn't give mere lip service to the skills of writing, speaking, and listening.
- all teachers outside the English Department would assign at least one essay during the course.
- all English teachers' loads were such that each teacher could know the name of each student before the end of the first marking period, and his needs before the end of the course.
- attorney generals didn't make declarations that a teacher on the State Board of Education would constitute a conflict of interest.
- teachers were only considered as competent as cosmetologists and morticians to determine their own certification.
- Boards of Education were only jailed or fined or forced back to work at the bargaining table too.
- administrators weren't forced by Boards of Education to do their bargaining against the enemy teacher during negotiations and be the teachers' leaders all the rest of the time.
- all the fresh, new, vital ideas weren't being lopped off with each year's crop of pink-slipping.

Halt! Consider only one more *if*. If you can't counterattack with any of the already stated militant ways against the inimical attitudes, and you can't find a way to put any of the *ifs* into practice, try one last alternative.

Alternative 4 (Activist)

The local teachers' union should use the methods the *good* citizens use to get elected to the Kiwanis presidency or to publicize the church bazaar. Individual teachers should become activists. Drop leaflets about school needs on doorsteps. Counteract community misinformation with mass mailings. Organize phone fan-outs to spread good news. Wear identifying green berets. Have drill teams ready for informational picket duty. Have Burma-Shave-spaced signs lead citizens to teacher-directed rap sessions. Man hot-line phones on a regular basis. March hundreds strong on every public school meeting. Bombard the press with letters to the editor if teachers' views are not being considered. Sport banners, bumper stickers, and buttons supporting teacher-initiated plans. Finally, carry off one giant PR extravaganza per year. No one can be hurt if activist teachers rent a zeppelin, hire a sky writer, and fly balloons with the message "Teachers Are Up for Kids."

The only constants in attitude in the last decade were ours: A problem had to become critical before we did; we didn't act but were reactionary; we always maneuvered defensively for fear of being offensive. We have used defensive alternatives. To put the fate of education back in our hands, not the failures of education on our backs, we need militant alternatives, united action.

To have pleasures outweigh the problems, we must make no more separate peaces.

The Demise of the
English Department

JONATHAN SWIFT

No high school department has had a more vital role to play in maintaining the human side of our existence in the face of depersonalization than the English Department. No department has had bloodier public battles for its very existence. Yet, like Humpty Dumpty, we English teachers are heading for a fracture from which we shall not emerge if we do not begin to look at the necessary evolution of this "English" department.

The term "English Department" is archaic; it is an anachronism. Our field of studies is no more "English" than it is exclusively "science fiction." Some say "language arts" is a better term but even this is inadequate. Others say our bag is "communication," a term that encompasses much more than traditional English, moving us into oral and media forms as well as literary. The name "communications" is significant; it reflects the attitudes within that department. Communication is vital; it is the essence of human relationships. It is an art as well as a skill to be acquired, but it is also a body of information to be studied. The arts of language form a vital part of human communication: Words paint dreams, help us make love, encourage us. These "language" arts, then, are in reality methods of communication: narratives, poetry, explanations, arguments found all around us. Using the term "communication" helps to emphasize that our task is global, that what we do in English class is not different in purpose from what language teachers do in China, Australia, Africa, and elsewhere on the globe. The job of the English teacher, then, is not simply to teach "English" but rather to show students the how, why, and what of communication and to cut them loose so that they can go about their business.

But the purpose of this particular essay is not simply to advocate a change of name for English departments. It is rather to make teachers aware of how little we have done in the past as English departments, how far we have to go to become strong, and what the consequences are of continued inactivity. I will want to consider several topics: the complexity of education today, the battle of the humanists and the "basicists," the expansion of educational alternatives (global education as an example), and the limitations of human and material resources. Finally, I will want to suggest some potential new directions for education which we could initiate starting tomorrow.

It is fortunate that today's exhausted teachers are still professionally interested in their work. We have emerged from an era of masochistic breast-beating, of public attacks transmitted through the media. We have changed somewhat, and we are tired, but we still continue to work on our curricula, and we will continue to do this because we cannot escape our nature: To be a teacher is to be an agent of change.

On one level American education appears to be changing today. The fifty states have been granted the power and the finances to control education. Michigan and California are nationally recognized leaders in the development of educational accountability models. Yet, as Robert Graham argues elsewhere in this book, the "delivery systems" of education have not appreciably changed. If we compare changes in the educational field to those in business, the sciences, or even religion, we are light years behind. Perhaps this is not surprising, for the areas now covered by "education" are mind-boggling. We are in an ever-expanding and ever-accelerating revolution. It has become increasingly difficult to define our jobs and our tasks. Furthermore, it is in the very nature of learning and knowledge that the boundaries of the disciplines will continue to blur and recede in the future. Little wonder that change comes slowly; it is difficult to see directions clearly.

The most important task facing curriculum experts today, it seems to me, is not the imparting of specific subject matter knowledge (something obsessing many state departments of education), but rather, teaching those special skills needed to acquire and apply the interrelated strands of knowledge for the future. The key term for our curriculum designers must be "pro-action," which implies that future events in education can be humanistically controlled by positive and planned action. Then we can all choose from among productive, reliable, funded alternatives.

Some critics have suggested that curriculum today is in a static stage due solely to the inactivity and alienation of teachers. There are many other reasons, however, for the reticence of high school teachers to press forward in curriculum. The proliferation of minicourses has led to a peculiar specialization which, instead of increasing teacher openness and mobility, has sharply decreased it. On the one hand, some schools have been looking for teachers who can teach science fiction, death, horror, philosophy, sports, and other typical categories with which teachers of yesteryear were but vaguely familiar. On the other hand, a significant number of schools are disenchanted with teachers who have compartmentalized, teachers who have narrowed, who have not expanded their pedagogical horizons.

The problem becomes even more acute for personnel departments and more discouraging for teachers in those areas of the country where student population is decreasing and fewer teachers are needed. National trends indicate these problems will worsen. Job insecurity is almost endemic to the profession. School districts are beginning to move teachers around as classrooms become empty. Curriculum supervisors are looking at the latest interpretations of low results on national tests. These interpretations agree on no one cause but suggest a combination of causes, including elective courses that may not offer as good preparation as writing and literature courses, and a reduction in the number of required courses in verbal skills. Considering all these problems, then, it is much easier to shift and/or hire a teacher for Secondary English 10, 11, or 12 where uniform drills and exercises abound than to shift and/or hire one who appears to have locked himself into a few minicourses from life to death.

To avoid retrogression we must make an honest assessment of the necessary skills and content for the young person heading toward the year 2000. We can no longer concern ourselves only with the pleasure of a course, but rather, we must consider the usefulness of it to the student. As teachers, we must "pro-act": We must adapt to the conditions of our environment. Our very existence as teachers depends on our recognizing one unassailable fact: The major part of life's learning does *not* take place in our schools. We must move out of the school, out of a narrow departmentalization that ignores the admittedly uncertified but certainly qualified expertise of the community. (After all, we have some admittedly unqualified but unfortunately certified teachers with unassailable tenure even within the schools.)

Beset by a yapping segment of the media and the public, we educators have been sidetracked into believing that a prolonged discussion of the "basics" is productive. It is not. Teachers in the field of communication arts should not be drawn into a debate about the "humanities" versus the "basics." We can learn from the history of education that "basics" include much more than the three Rs. And that statement in no way minimizes the clear importance of reading and writing.

It is estimated that, for every book a student reads, he views twenty or thirty films. *Via* a series of films, people can sit back and watch unfold the ascent of the species through all the great civilizations of the past in one great color spectacle—contained in a small box. Yet this modern miracle of media is not even in the hands of those responsible for formal education. I want to argue that the word "basic" in education should be expanded. Do we mean basic to being human, basic to the ability to communicate, create, synthesize? Skills such as word usage, conventions, and punctuation are only a small part of what the communication teacher is about. Those skills are only carriers; they have *no* significance in themselves. (It is appalling to consider that there are still some teachers who equate "good" writing with error-free writing.) Since the present and future generations will be exposed more and more to media and retrieval systems, educators have a professional duty to pro-act. What *is* being done by schools to aid students in the acquisition of those skills relative to media production, analysis, criticism? In the school community, the instructional materials center is becoming an extension of the communication arts and should increasingly be used as such.

At least part of the task of a teacher in communication arts involves an examination of the nature of human beings. For ages we have done this through literature, and we must renew our determination to inculcate freedom of expression and interpretation. "There are no answers, only questions," said the sage. The job of a communications teacher is to present people responding to their own questions in books, poems, art.

Yet there is also a reality ethos for the future. This demands that teachers confront the reality of controversy, hate, and violence if they want to help young people understand human nature—on a personal, national, or international scale. It is the role of the imagination and of creative literature to extend our students' experiences of personal social contacts to international relationships. And there is more. While there is a built-in obsolescence in the evolution of scientific and mathematical theories, literature and other arts are cumulative. They form a body of knowledge that reflects generations of wisdom in history from one corner of the globe to another. This body of knowledge must be studied to be understood.

All this, in turn, takes money. We need money to run our business. American education is a staggering financial enterprise. Even the federal government gives billions of dollars to an enterprise supposedly funded by the states. Total education expenditures in the 1980s will probably rise beyond $150 billion. American education expenditures alone account for about 8 percent of the Gross National Product. Yet despite all this cash, we know that school districts from California to New York are becoming more and more strapped for funds, have no monies for teacher in-service courses, curriculum improvement, innovation in methodology, and student field trips. Education, then, will increasingly require an aggressive creativity in the search for financial support.

The answer to this immense problem of financial support probably lies in two activities: looking at our fundamental educational goals, then asking ourselves what funded programs can be tailored to meet these goals. Often the federal- and state-funded programs represent an alternative emphasis rather than an attempt to thwart fundamental goals. There is nothing essentially harmful in state or federal agencies providing extrinsic motivation to increase our intrinsic motivation. It is continually surprising how flexible these funded programs can be. There has been money for teachers' in-service courses, curriculum innovation and renovation, and instructional materials for the communication arts coming out of Career Education, Global Education, Bilingual Education, Bicultural Education, Values Education, Ethnic Studies, Community Education, Parent and Student Involvement Studies, Humanities, and other funded programs. Rather than becoming paranoid about federal or state intervention, rather than sitting around and complaining, teachers should decide precisely what they want to do, then look around for the funds. Every district should hire an expert whose sole task it is to keep up with state and federal funding and to communicate this to the entire educational community.

The alternatives to "English" are many, and each has its own worth. I want to examine one of these, *Global Education.* Briefly, Global Education calls for a curriculum that will involve students in cultural, scientific, ecological, and economic issues that affect everyone. It promotes an understanding of the values and priorities of the many cultures of the world, as well as the basic concepts and principles related to world communities. It can offer a vital combination of language, literature, and the arts of many cultures. It includes all the traditional values of "English," that literature and language are a reflection of people, their values and needs, their enemies and heroes, and that language is the living instrument of communication. Global Education aims to increase student awareness of cultural, political, and economic interdependence in the world of the past, present, and future. The schools have split humanity into disciplines, losing sight of the law of synergism that a system can be greater than the sum of its "departmental" parts. The cross-cultural, comparative, and interdisciplinary approach of Global Education offers a useful alternative. English teachers, as well as scientists and social scientists, would do well to become familiar with the holistic ideas of Buckminster Fuller and Alexander Bronowski, with the imagination and perception of Isaac Asimov. Just as grammar has no value *in itself,* literature has no value in itself. It becomes valuable only when we see it as a mirror of our humanity—our aspirations, our sorrows, our joys. It is when we see literature as the creative product of a human being who strove to communicate his soul that we appreciate the beauty of his work. Literature tells us what it can mean to be a person—whether an ancient Roman, Oriental, Indian, or African. Only then are we prepared to ask *ourselves* what it means to be a person, and finally an *American* person facing the year 2000.

The very nature of human curiosity demands that we seek beyond our own world and communicate with others all that we find. The dilemma in which we now find ourselves is the dichotomy between our own ethnic, national, or local traditions and the rapidly expanding world of technology and instant communication that has, in fact, shrunk the globe. We can instantly retrieve economic statistics ruling our lives, but individuals cannot so easily retrieve their self-identity or collective unconscious.

The attempt of Global Education to solve this problem would center on interdisciplinary courses: Early World Literature and Other Creative Arts; World History and Earth Science; American Arts, History, and Government; Two Hundred Years of Scientific Discovery Reflected in Literature of the Time; Modern Science Fiction, Physics, and Computer Science. Team taught, these courses can begin to reflect, on more than an elementary level, the oneness of human beings, of all ages, colors, and parts of the globe.

The same kind of rationale might be attempted for many of the alternatives in education. Each of them can be called a "delivery system" for special skills and knowledge vital to *one* group of students, an approach by *one* group of teachers. Basic to all, however, is communication. Why, then, should not we in the communication arts take full advantage of *all* these alternatives for the sake of our students and ourselves?

Because of pressures from many sources, withdrawal of revenues, and our job insecurities, we have become defensive. We tend to dismiss summarily any new alternatives as fads. In fact, we have become distrustful to the point that the teacher who wishes to innovate is suspect, the administrator who has the nerve to meddle in curriculum is undermined, the parent who offers suggestions is merely tolerated. Yet education is unquestionably a community endeavor. No teacher can do it alone.

In spite of, or perhaps because of, the pain we have suffered from the attacks of national magazines and other "inflammatory" publications, we have learned that much of our poor public relations may have been deserved. We have also learned that there *are* individuals outside the profession who are wise and creative in matters of education. We have learned by opening the classroom closet that much of what happens under the guise of innovation is, in fact, retrenchment. Finally, we have learned that there are, indeed, many paths to learning that may be equally effective. All of what we have learned points to alternatives—from alternative educational institutions to alternative curricula, methodology, evaluation, and goals.

Fundamentally, I am arguing for total change in the structure and curriculum delivery of the present high school English department. The essence of the thesis is, "Change or die." Today's and tomorrow's needs are not served by yesterday's systems. At the same time, this does not suggest a change in the basic concepts of education any more than it suggests that basic human values have changed since the ancient Greeks. I am advocating change so that:

1. Skills and knowledge are treated as a totality, not as single disciplines.
2. The school expands into the community for human and material resources.
3. Students and teachers adopt alternative ways of learning.
4. Fundamental skills, awareness, knowledge are sedulously taught through a variety of emphases.
5. Parent and student dialogue in curriculum building and evaluation is increased.
6. Teachers go out of their departments, even out of the school into the educational community.
7. New methods of educational financing are found.

If we can achieve this, we will be prepared for the year 2000. But this will also require a change in that monolithic dodo, the English Department. One cannot help but feel some regret at the passing of this giant. However, when we see clearly the transition to another state more in keeping with its evolutionary and traditional goals, it is time for rejoicing. The Secondary School English Department is dead! Long live the Un-School of Communication Arts!

Given the knowledge we now have, the trends and processes that have already begun, the future is really not as mysterious and unpredictable as it first appears. To stimulate some thought, here, then, are a few considerations that might affect departments in the next ten or fifteen years.

1. The phasing out of the traditional *English Department* and the emphasis on *communication* arts: writing, speech, music, literature, drama, fine arts, etc.
2. Even more expression of "anti-establishment" behavior in sup-

port of rights for individuals and minorities—lobbying against grouping, grading, behavioral objectives, etc.

3. A process of learning that emphasizes *not* compliance but the individual's alternatives.
4. Reduced language arts graduation requirements.
5. Increased alternatives for high school completion.
6. Increased use of proficiency tests to "opt out" of requirements.
7. Increased accountability in all basic skills and subject matter knowledge.
8. Increased community participation in the educational process.
9. An increase in self-awareness, personal growth progress, and humanism.
10. Increased use and refinement of instructional media, retrieval and replication systems.
11. Decreased reliance on system-wide adoption of texts.
12. A "flattening out" of dogmatic ethical peaks and valleys.
13. Declining high school population.
14. Increased involuntary teacher movement within districts.
15. Increased teacher union pressures: greater concern with job protection than curriculum.
16. Expanded career (awareness and experiential) opportunities within the curriculum.
17. Teachers as roving consultants working with the community.
18. Increased student power, organization, and curricular involvement.
19. Continued evolution of legal precedents in education.
20. Acceptance and involvement of the educational community of many models of instructional accountability and monitored educational achievement.
21. Increase in international interaction, in the teaching of foreign languages and foreign literature in translation.
22. Increase in the status of educators proportionate to the increased effectiveness of evaluation procedures and community interaction.
23. Development of a national network of procedures.
24. Federally sponsored teacher training centers.

The future of the secondary school language arts department is *not* out of the hands of chairpersons and teachers. The future will become what our educational community desires and wills it to be. Consequently, we must with great deliberation decide where we are going to apply our pressures, our creativity, and our hard work, and what we are going to adopt as our educational and social goals.

Dialogue:
The Contributors Respond

It would be pleasant to report that the following dialogue among the authors of this volume took place during a three-day conference at the spacious country retreat of Edu-Think, Incorporated, a private non-profit organization devoted exclusively to the support and development of literacy studies or that it was funded by the U.S. Office of Education. Alas, I cannot. The dialogue that follows took place under the benign sponsorship of the U.S. Postal Service with federal "aid" in the form of postage stamps, which *we* purchased. [S.N.J.]

Stan Cook notes that "few, if any, of today's experimental modes have sprung full blown upon the American educational system." Frank Ross describes "progress" using the metaphor of a coiled spring, suggesting that we keep coming back to the same place in education, just a little further along. Bob Graham asserts that the English taught in the schools today differs only in surface appearance from that advocated by the Committee of Ten in 1894. What is your sense of the progress (or lack of it) in English in this century? As we move toward the future, what can we learn from our past?

Henry Maloney

I think you'd have to say there has been "progress" in a great many areas. Today's public school graduates are better prepared in English than students of twenty-five years ago were, irrespective of some test results, but English teachers can take only partial credit for the improvement. Today's young people have had broader social and literary experiences because they are far more likely to have had an opportunity to discuss the works of black writers. Moreover, young people who graduate today have had an opportunity to get to know and enjoy books from the "real world," since the kinds of paperback books they can purchase at a nearby shopping center have been introduced to them in school.

The "classics" no longer dominate the curriculum. Although each one of today's students may not have taken part in making a film, as a group they are more apt to have seen kids make films, or, at least, to have seen a film made by kids. So far, I have suggested that today's graduates may be better equipped because of social and technological changes, but the impact of such changes on what is taught must be reckoned with. All in all, I would say that today's English programs have become less "school-ish," less oriented toward a this-is-the-way-we-do-it-in-school and the-rest-of-the-world-is-wrong philosophy. One need not infer that abandoning schoolish ·English has caused language to become more cliché-ridden, more imprecise, more carelessly used. There is a middle ground between scholarly excess and slovenly excess that English teachers are aiming toward.

Jean Malmstrom

As my article suggests, I'm afraid I see little real progress in the English taught in the schools today. The more it changes, the more it seems to remain the same. I was interested that several of the other contributors expressed essentially the same opinion.

Stanley Cook

The easiest way to teach is as one was taught; by this means, good and bad teaching persist in about the same proportion from generation to generation. Too many teachers take advanced courses only for credit or for salary increments. Those who attend conferences and who listen are those who least need to do so. The same applies to membership in professional organizations such as NCTE. The greatest progress occurs when a sincere staff has time together. Conant's four sections [of English] and one hundred students would allow such cross fertilization as no perfunctory after-school workshops for tired teachers could effect. This happened only *one year* in Grosse Pointe High School in all the years that I taught there.

Jonathan Swift

In the past quarter of a century, national and international commentators on education earned a lot more than their daily bread giving us doomsday warnings about the necessary change that must take place in the educational system. It is not a matter, however, that changes will have to be made in our schools; it is a matter that changes have to *continue* to be made. The essence of any dynamic institution is its willingness to improve, using what evolution is necessary. To bring about this acceptance of a dynamic educational condition as a natural fact requires courage, stamina, strong feelings of ego-support, and faith on the part of educators. Essentially, we are in a *condition* now no different from the one we were in when the public railroaded Socrates into doing himself in because he was teaching the dynamics of change. Too many commentators today delude themselves into believing that they actually have something radically different to say. Ho-hum! Education will continue to change its garments—not radically—but slowly with fads and fancies, and ups and downs. It will be, however, those quiet courageous teachers who are dynamic yet deliberate, curious yet faithful, optimistic yet realistic, who will change the system from the inside out.

Pat Fox observes that for much of the past decade "a problem had to become critical before we did; we didn't act, but were reactionary." Given all the attacks on English teachers, which, if any, seem to you to have validity? If we had had our own professional "watchdog" committee during the past decade or two, what might it have brought to our attention?

Frank Ross

What we have needed is not a professional watchdog committee, but a pool of South American piranha into which we could dunk school administrators, school board members, and occasional influential citizens who have nearly destroyed the teaching of English by two actions: (1) by diluting the English curriculum with extraneous studies that don't seem to fit into any other department but seem appropriate to English because they happen to have the course of study written in that language, e.g. career education (what ninth grade is now without it?); (2) by diminishing the teacher's hours of effectiveness by adding to the business of classroom teaching such arcane subjects as study hall, lunch duty, hallguard, and the shuffling of reams of administrative paper. Piranha may be too good for them. How about a cage of African killer bees?

Stan Cook

I'm not certain teachers *are* willing to police themselves. As a whole they are docile or just plain scared. A few years ago we in Michigan were polled concerning a new tenure law. In school after school the vote went 100 percent in favor of the principal's view, whatever that was. Schools side by side in the same system had opposite votes. Wasn't that shameful? Associations and federations and subject matter departments should be forums for meeting and anticipating internal and external challenges. If teachers dared state their case, they might just be heard!

Jonathan Swift

Had we honestly assessed our limitations in the 1960s, we would have realized there are parental and community roles that we, as teachers, cannot fulfill. Articulating more clearly in a united fashion what we *were* about, we might have headed off adverse public criticism regarding behavioral and attitudinal areas over which we had no control. Yet, because those areas impinged upon the classroom, we passively accepted responsibility and acted selectively, often injudiciously. In the area of professional leadership, large numbers of us have fallen into unionism. At its best, this means a hypersensitive awareness of accountability, teaching conditions, teacher/student ratios, administrative harassment, job security, and self-serving preoccupations. At worst, it means an erosion of vital interests in the intellectual pursuits of students and teachers, of the confluent aspects of curriculum. While I recognize the necessity of job negotiation, I fear the creation of a monster that must grow in power just to exist.

> **Mildred Webster makes a strong case for including classic literature in the curriculum, yet even she acknowledges that students "will probably be less book-minded" in the future. What do you see as the future of literature in the schools? Of literary study in general?**

Pat Fox

I love literature and love to teach literature. So does every other English teacher. That's one of the things *wrong* with English teaching methods these days. We need to instigate our own variety of affirmative action: Eliminate the study of literature at all levels—elementary through grad school—and require prospective English teachers (and current English teachers?) all to take skills courses in thinking, writing, reading, speaking, and listening and courses in how to teach the skills to others. When the skills and thinking have caught up to the level of literature study, only then would it be returned to English curricula. With literature in the curriculum at all levels as it is now, nothing modest will dislodge it.

Robert Graham

Today, as in the past, we teach content. We teach students to read and then, perversely, to explicate for the teacher. This is in the print tradition established by the printing press. No other book has profited more from Gutenberg's invention than the Bible. Before the printing press the Bible was interpreted in conformity with an oral tradition available only to a trained elite. The printing press made the Reformation possible, because then all could read the text and interpret it in the light of individual conscience. Schools have never seriously studied the process by which thought is molded by the act of making it print. I have the feeling that in the future we will pay more attention to the processes by which we communicate and how these processes influence our messages. A play on the boards is different in message from its printed form, which, in turn, differs from the film, which also differs from the radio and TV versions. To these communication processes can be added computers and videophones, and one doesn't really know what next. The proper use of the computer in the classroom is not for drill and practice but to teach computer literacy—that is, to teach how the computer works physically, and then to learn how to communicate with it, and then to come to understand how the process of using a computer influences the act of communicating. Not much of this is done now, but I feel that attention to the study of *process* will come to replace literature study just as English and American literature replaced Greek and Latin.

Henry Maloney

I hope that the future of literature is not as bleak as it appears to be in the final scene of the film version of *Fahrenheit 451*. In Truffaut's movie, a colony of zombie-like people pace around memorizing textbooks, apparently to show the audience that there is hope for the survival of ideas. Ironically, these survivors of the book culture are so engrossed in the process of memorizing the classics that they seem to have lost their humanity. I don't think that a group of walking libraries solves the problem of preserving literary values if they have not preserved the vitality and inspirational qualities great literature offers. If there is not room in four years of high school education for students to chew and digest at least a half dozen great, enduring books from the past, then a link to some earlier realities that students must reckon with in their lifetimes becomes badly damaged.

Jean Malmstrom's "Future Grammar" is, in effect, a curriculum based on modern linguistics. Do you see "linguistic" attitudes toward language and language study playing a greater role in the curriculum than they do now?

Jean Malmstrom

Despite my "call" in the essay, I do not see "linguistic attitudes toward language and language study" playing a greater role in the curriculum than they do now, even as I work for that result. My main reason is that teachers too often are so inadequately educated in linguistics and linguistic attitudes that they lack the knowledge and self-confidence required for such liberated teaching.

Robert Graham

Linguistics in the classroom, college or school, is nearly always the linguistics of the printed page. It calls our attention to written English. But written English is only a dialect of living spoken English, and the study of that language involves not only syntactics but also phonology. Children today are not as print-oriented as we. Their metaphors are composed in sight and sound. The study and application of phonology are more appropriate to the thinking and communication of present and future generations. I should think that one of these days there will be a flurry of activity in the applications of phonologic insight. Edmund Carpenter points out, "The new mass media—film, radio, TV—are new languages, their grammars as yet unknown." My son Paul asked me the meaning of a word I had used with him in a conversation. After I had explained and illustrated the meaning, Paul said, "You saw that word in your head like on TV, didn't you?" I didn't, but I think he does.

Frank Ross

Sorry, Jean. I never could agree with you on anything. (Chomsky, yes.) I see the complete extinction of grammar by 2001 in the secondary schools. If one looks really closely in the schools today he sees that there are a lot of grammar books—old and new grammar—being purchased, but almost none are being taught. At the university level, grammar may just be moved into the philosophy department, along with thralls, dominions, and seraphim. Just exactly how many angels can *sit* on the head of a pin?

Pat Fox

My radical suggestion is to eliminate all foreign language teaching in the schools for a period of time, so that English language in the schools is not seen by the elitists as "basic" to the study of foreign languages. Who knows, maybe even some English teachers would become convinced that English isn't Latin.

Geneva Smitherman declares that teaching dialects is a political act, whether one chooses to impose a standard dialect or not. Recent court cases show that teaching dialect has become a legal issue, and a teacher may be sued (though not necessarily with success) for not teaching standard English. What do you see happening in the "politics of correctness" in coming years? Do students have a right to their own language?

Jonathan Swift

If the court legislates the teaching of language, there had better be a check-and-balance system—another "learned" body (à l'Acadèmie Francaise) that will decide on what is acceptable language and what is due to eccentricity or carelessness. Rather than a judicial rigmarole that would be linguistically repugnant to many, perhaps we can increase our focus on the concept of *appropriateness*. We have two parallels: One is the central European who speaks several dialects and doesn't use any one at the wrong time; the other is the area of written composition wherein teachers have directed a written work to an audience showing students the necessary adaptations for each audience. As a parent and/or teacher I would want my child to be capable of adapting in writing and speaking. His language reserves would be poor indeed if he used the mode of expression in the dining room during a football scrimmage, and vice versa.

Robert Graham

If our students are segregated in their language interactions, then English becomes a second or perhaps a standard foreign language. It isn't so much a matter of students having a "right" to their own language as having a right to be *themselves*. "Correctness" in the classroom usually means "politeness" in a middle-class register, but dialects are also "correct" in the appropriate context.

Stan Cook

Standard English is not a political issue, nor is it a moral one. A standard dialect is with us, not because it was ever imposed but because it is functional. Yiddish was functional in the ghetto, but not outside. Pennsylvania Dutch sufficed on the farm, but with land prices what they are, some of the Amish younger sons must find work among the worldly. What one speaks at home or on the street is a privilege the state should not deny him. But he also has the right to learn the standard dialect so that he may survive in today's complicated economic world.

Looking into his "Plexiglas ball," Frank Ross sees technological advances and administrative cost consciousness combining to create a split between basic skills courses taught to all students and elective courses in the humanities, taught by specialists to large numbers of students. Do you see this as a likely direction for English? Are there other ways in which technology and the economy may shape our discipline?

Pat Fox

Frank Ross's Plexiglas ball is really reflecting the *present*. Come on, Frank, get a real crystal ball and tell us what's going to happen next.

Stan Cook

Mechanical skills can be taught mechanically, either by machines or by teaching specialists. Used properly, the devices might release human beings to teach human values to small groups and to individual students.

Jonathan Swift

It is in the evolutionary nature of our educational system to complicate itself. Now we have to add technological and administrative considerations to all our pedagogical deliberations. There is a danger here to which we must be alert. There is a limit to what individual teachers or even groups of teachers can do. Like the total profession, English teachers have a tendency to bite off more than they can chew. The result is they volunteer to become accountable for a complexity of responsibilities they can never meet because many of these responsibilities should—although they may not—be met by others more appropriately designated by training or role.

Ken Macrorie suggests in his conversation with John Bennett that every good teacher teaches his or her *self*, rather than a set body of facts or skills. Do you agree? Is there room for such a teacher in today's and tomorow's schools?

Robert Graham

Why separate the teacher from the skills to be taught? When I taught my younger son how to safely operate the lawnmower last summer, I tried to do it in such a way that he not only learned but enjoyed learning. That is my way, and if it takes, we are both satisfied and successful. When I work with a student in the classroom, I do it in the same way. The two former teachers of mine at South Hills High that I referred to in my contribution were successful in that with me. The skills and feelings they synthesized were a personal mix of what they were as people and what they thought was best and necessary for us. What is best and necessary today is different. The mixing is still the same, personal. For that there always was and always will be a need.

Ken Macrorie

In that interview, John and I spent a disproportionate time on the matter of truthtelling because we—and other teachers we know— have found that an effort for truth is the key that unlocks not only the telling incident, the order of parts of a story which creates suspense and meaning, but fresh expression, original metaphor, rhythms, and other sound effects that do more than enhance what is being said— that in fact make what is said what it is. We have learned that writing is partly a conscious and partly an unconscious process. That is why John says so much about the teacher being truthful and not posing before the class. He is not teaching *himself;* he is teaching writing. But I should not say it that way, for it indicates but one of the two opposites that must be demonstrated. Out there in that space between teacher and student they must fuse themselves and their disciplines and produce energy that can be used.

Frank Ross

I am certain Macrorie mainly teaches himself rather than a body of facts or skills. And may his numbers multiply. That good teachers do indeed do this is the one hope of salvation for our country. In our diversity we may nurture frustrations but that diversity represents the only real strength for a democracy. Anyone who says otherwise has misread the Federalist papers, or instead read Barbara Cartland. Mark Hopkins on one end of a log still lives in the classrooms of English teachers who have come to grips with their own problems and have a clear concept of what kind of leadership young people seek and need. Those young people with those Macrorie-like teachers won't look for their models in hairy English punks strumming reputed instruments. Such teachers are the first to be pinkslipped when the budget feels a pain, or, if they have tenure, they are usually the ones ridiculed and harrassed by an administration that seeks only conformists to teach a monolithic curriculum.

Bob Graham asserts that power over the curriculum has largely shifted into the hands of lawmakers. Are teachers merely the

"implementors" of legal decisions and funding acts? What is the future of this kind of curriculum? Who's in charge here, anyway?

Frank Ross

Bob Graham hath spoke. In our capitalist society the one who pays the piper has always called the tune. Previously ignorant school boards have allowed teachers to write the curriculum as long as it didn't tell the truth about Jefferson's sleeping with slave girls or Oscar Wilde's consuming desire to get to the end of things. As our bad luck would have it, just as school boards are beginning to be staffed with genuinely interested, caring, real people, the source of funding has now shifted out of the community to an even more ignorant, mendacious legislature. And they will have the curriculum that their combined blind spots can etch, with the help of leader-dog-lobbyists, of course.

Jean Malmstrom

I'm afraid I have to agree with Bob. Teachers feud so constantly and idiosyncratically among themselves that they characteristically offer no united leadership. Moreover, lawmakers control the money without which very little can be accomplished. Thus, in fact, lawmakers are in charge, and the future looks discouraging.

Stan Cook

Everybody has gone to school. Therefore everybody—even a legislator—is an expert on education. During the depression there was a movement toward making schools the agent for a planned society. That radical scheme faded, but we now have piecemeal attacks, amendments, pressures, censorings, and imposed responsibilities from all directions. And the days aren't any longer. As the role of the family declines, that of the school increases, in spite of the intense competition for student time and student attention in today's world. I am suspicious of any system—Skinner's, Marx's, or anybody's—which orders our lives. Democratic education should release the individual's potential, not manipulate it.

Jonathan Swift

One of the most insidious errors we teach in the United States today is that our country is *the* nation of legal freedoms. Freedom takes many forms and many countries excel: the United Kingdom, Sweden, Switzerland, Australia, and many others. It appears to me that in our manic search for *individual* freedoms we have shifted focus from some of the communal values and ethics necessary to a viable society. It is as guides toward individualism tempered by these communal values that teachers should appear. While becoming aware of the new legal nuances and clarifications that affect us daily, we must not lose sight of our historically American human values and discipline which must supersede individual desires and whims from the points of view of both teacher and learner. Besides this, there is an *active* legal role that teachers can take. Part of our responsibility as educators is to advise and "bird-dog" legislators in all matters regarding education. Since new laws are inescapable, we should advise on necessary funding, and we should protest injudicious assessment programs. We are accountable to laws: we must, therefore, take a hand in shaping them.

> **Jon Swift prophesies the demise of the English department as interdisciplinary studies increasingly absorb our attention. Others have predicted the death of English for such diverse reasons as the lack of customers to the incompetence of the practitioners (teachers). Are we, as our Editor at Hayden, Bob Boynton, has suggested, "looking more and more dodoish" all the time? What, if anything, can the profession do now to control its own fate?**

Pat Fox

I'm in a destructive frame of mind. I would like to throw out literature, foreign languages, and now English departments. Instead of departments of English, require that a percentage (large) of every other department be trained as English teachers first and only secondarily in the content area. Eliminate English requirements for students, but have a percentage (large) of the content area grade be based upon the student's ability to comprehend the ideas of that discipline and communicate them in discussions and in written form. While we're at it, why not shoot (or retrain) every teacher who stands behind a podium more than 20 percent of the time?

Jean Malmstrom

I disagree with Jon. I think that high school English departments will continue to exist but will reflect increasingly the already highly visible trend in college English departments to return to their former service function as teachers of writing, and of whatever else is popularly considered relevant to its improvement. The SAT scores continue to frighten the taxpayers, and the schools cannot exist without financial support. We can rationalize all we wish, but we are largely talking to ourselves, not to the people out there.

Stan Cook

If teachers of everything else were literate readers and writers and spoke the language with precision, English teachers would be expendable. Such was an observation made by Rollo LaVerne Lyman, a President of the NCTE back in the 1930s. That solution has yet to come about, but it might. Two of the finest writing teachers I have known taught ninth grade civics.

Henry Maloney

Presently there is more that should be taught in English classes than the secondary school program can comfortably provide time for, and this body of knowledge and skills is constantly expanding as contemporary writers, filmmakers, and others continue to produce and as scholars gain additional insights into the nature and function of language. It is my belief that some of the needed focus on using words with precision and on writing well-organized compositions would be lost if English programs lost their identity. Further, I see teacher training for a secondary "humanities department" emphasizing a little learning about several things instead of providing substantial preparation in one field. Superficial preparation can weaken the teaching-learning process for potential teachers and for students. We should strongly encourage the English teacher to relate literature to the other arts and to the ideas of appropriate thinkers, but we should not obscure the fundamental need to teach communication processes by taking away the English teacher's identity.

Bob Graham

You asked what can we do to control our fate. I feel we are faced with the "snail darter" syndrome: That the small species should cease to exist is not important; but should we not defend it, then we may lose control of our environment and lose much that is good and beautiful in our lives, if not life itself. That *Julius Caesar* should cease to be part of the English curriculum is not important, but should we cease to defend what is good and beautiful and human in language, then we may lose that insight and become skill processors. Socrates pointed out the evils of the written word and its pernicious influence upon oral thought, and by early modern times his point was borne out. Now as captives of printed thought we rail at the new media of communication. Had Plato not written down Socratic thought we would have lost it, and I suggest that without electronic media our thought may be lost to our heirs. We, like Socrates, are too much one with our environment to see it for what it is. We must develop the vision to see beyond it.

About the Authors

STEPHEN JUDY is professor of English, Michigan State University, and editor of *The English Journal.* He has been a director of the Secondary Section of the National Council of Teachers of English and a member of the Executive Committee of the Conference on English Education. He is a past president of the Michigan Council of Teachers of English and a recipient of the Council's Charles Carpenter Fries Award for service in the teaching of English. His books include *Explorations in the Teaching of Secondary English, Writing in Reality, The Creative Word, Lecture Alternatives in Teaching English,* and *The ABCs of Literacy.*

FRANK E. ROSS is a member of the faculty of Eastern Michigan University. He has been a contributing editor to *Media and Methods* magazine. A past president of the Michigan Council of Teachers of English, he has long been active in the National Council of Teachers of English as well.

M. ROBERT GRAHAM is Associate Director for English with the Oakland Schools, Pontiac, Michigan. He is editor of *Alternative Strategy in the Teaching of English,* former editor of *The Michigan English Teacher,* a contributor to *The English Journal,* and a frequent speaker at national meetings. He has taught junior high school, senior high school, and college courses in Michigan.

STANLEY COOK has taught all grades from fifth (in a two-room country school) to graduate course assignments at Wayne State University. The bulk of his teaching was at Grosse Pointe (Michigan) High School, where he was English Department head for twenty years. Long active in both MCTE and NCTE, he was on the NCTE Secondary Committee from 1966 to 1969. He received the Charles Carpenter Fries Award of the Michigan Council in 1974 and retired from active teaching in 1974, after forty-five years in the classroom.

KEN MACRORIE is emeritus professor of English, Western Michigan University, and has been editor of *College Composition and Communication.* His books include *Uptaught, A Vulnerable Teacher, Telling Writing,* and *Writing to Be Read.* He writes a column on teaching for *Media and Methods.*

JOHN BENNETT teaches at Kalamazoo Central High School, Kalamazoo, Michigan. He has been a member of the Commission on Composition of the National Council of Teachers of English and the Executive Committee of the Michigan Council of Teachers of English, for whom he served as a liaison with the Michigan Council for the Arts.

HENRY B. MALONEY is currently an associate professor of education at the University of Detroit. He taught in elementary and secondary schools before becoming a supervisor of secondary English for the Detroit Public Schools. A past president of the Michigan Council of Teachers of English, he has served on various committees and edited three books for the National Council of Teachers of English: *Accountability and the Teaching of English; New English, New Imperatives;* and *Behavioral Objectives and the Teaching of English.*

MILDRED WEBSTER has taught high school in North Dakota, in Ironwood, Michigan, and in St. Joseph, Michigan. She served the Michigan Council of Teachers of English as its treasurer, secretary, vice president, membership secretary, and executive secretary and has three times been given citations for work on behalf of the Council. Active in the National Council as well, she was co-chair of the Department Chairman Conference, chair of the Secondary Section, and a member of the NCTE Executive Board.

JEAN MALMSTROM is emeritus professor of English at Western Michigan University, which gave her its Alumni Award for Teaching Excellence, and a past president of the Michigan Council, which honored her with its Charles Carpenter Fries Award for distinguished service to the profession. Active in NCTE as well, she has served on the College Section Committee and chaired the College Section Summer Conference. Her publications include *Understanding Language: A Primer for the Language Arts Teacher; Grammar Basics: A Reading/Writing Approach; Dialects U.S.A.; Language in Society;* and *Who's Afraid of Linguistics?*

GENEVA SMITHERMAN is director of the Center for Black Studies and associate professor of Speech Communication at Wayne State University in Detroit. She is the author of *Talkin' and Testifyin': The Language of Black America* and an award-winning column, "Soul 'N Style," for *The English Journal.* Her teaching experience includes the Detroit Public Schools, Harvard University, Eastern Michigan University, and the University of Michigan. She has served on the NCTE Commission on Curriculum and on the Executive Committee of the Conference on

College Composition and Communication and was a member of the Task Force that produced the NCTE resolution and subsequent publication, "The Students' Right to Their Own Language."

PATRICIA W. FOX teaches at Grosse Pointe North High School in Michigan, where she has served as interdisciplinary writing consultant. A frequent speaker at professional meetings on state and national levels, she has also contributed articles to *The English Journal*.

JONATHAN SWIFT is department chair at Stevenson High School, Livonia, Michigan. An author of several *English Journal* articles, he has served as chair of the Conference of Secondary School English Department Chairpersons (CSSEDC) of NCTE and has been a member of the Secondary Section Committee. A frequent presenter at state conferences, he has also been a vice president of the Michigan Council of Teachers of English.